Bernadette Brennan is a Lecturer in Australian Literature at the University of Sydney. She gained her PhD from that institution in 2001 and was awarded the Eva Veronika Vidak Memorial Prize for the best thesis on an Australian topic. Bernadette's research interest is in the field of Literature and Ethics. She has published widely in *Australian Literary Studies*, *JASAL*, *Southerly*, *Antipodes* and *The Round Table: The Commonwealth Journal of International Affairs*, *Departures: How Australia Reinvents Itself* (MUP 2002), *Australian Literature and the Public Sphere* (ASAL 1998) and *Australian Writing and the City* (ASAL 1999). She has co-edited *JASAL* (2005) and *Southerly* (2007) and is on the Editorial Board for *Studies in Australasian Cinema*. Bernadette is currently working on a critical study of Brian Castro's writing.

JUST WORDS?

AUSTRALIAN AUTHORS WRITING FOR JUSTICE

Edited by Bernadette Brennan

UQP

First published 2008 by University of Queensland Press
PO Box 6042, St Lucia, Queensland 4067 Australia

www.uqp.uq.edu.au

Typeset in 11/16pt Minion Regular by Post Pre-press Group, Brisbane
Printed in Australia by McPherson's Printing Group

Australia Council for the Arts

This project has been assisted by the Commonwealth Government through the Australia Council, its arts funding and advisory body.

Cataloguing-in-Publication Data
National Library of Australia
Just words? Australian authors writing for justice.

ISBN 978 0 7022 3638 9 (pbk.).

1. Australian literature - History and criticism. 2. Justice in literature. 3. Ethics in literature. 4. Social change in literature. 5. Australia - In literature. I. Brennan, Bernadette.

820.9994

For Noel

Contents

Introduction

'The chief glory of every people arises from its authors.'
Samuel Johnson, Preface to the *Dictionary*

Questions about the writer's role in, and influence on, society are not new. Samuel Johnson, writing in 1755, identified writers as 'propagators of knowledge', as 'teachers of truth'. He saw his work, in compiling the English dictionary, as being worthwhile if it helped spread writers' words across nations and through time. While writers create with the hope that their words will affect readers and listeners, there is no way of measuring where their writing will surface or how that writing will influence its audience. Australian writing has always engaged with ethical and social issues. There has been, however, a marked resurgence over the last decade of writing interested in the relationship between texts and their social, political and ethical contexts and meanings. Interestingly, this turn to ethics is both a national and an international phenomenon.

The rationale for this collection is that after many years of conservative federal government, of more concentrated and controlled media ownership and of ever-shrinking arts funding, increasing numbers of Australian writers seem to be taking it upon themselves to encourage imaginative, constructive understanding of issues to do with moral, social, political and legal justice. The success of publications such as *Griffith Review*, *Quarterly Essay* and *The Monthly*, and the increasing popularity of writers' festivals which promote discussion about the relationship between writing and the way we live our lives, suggests that there is a growing Australian readership eager to engage with writing about these issues.

Significantly, this turn to ethics is occurring at a time when, it has been argued, Australian society is becoming less compassionate, less tolerant. In his latest book, *Advance Australia . . . Where?* (Hachette, Australia, 2007), social researcher Hugh McKay labels the last ten years in Australia as the 'Dreamy Period': a time when Australians, in the face of uncertainty, retreated or disengaged from big-picture questions of national security, immigration and war and focused instead on the minutiae of suburban life. At the same time, novels by Eva Sallis, Tom Keneally, Richard Flanagan, Andrew McGahan and Brian Castro, essays by Raimond Gaita, Robert Manne, Inga Clendinnen and Noel Pearson, non-fiction works such as David Marr and Marion Wilkinson's *Dark Victory* (2003), Version 1.0 productions of 'CMI – A Certain Maritime Incident' (2003) and 'Unfinished Business: X Marks the Spot', and films like Clara Law's *Letters to Ali* (2004) and Khoa Do's *The Finished People* (2003), indicate that Australian writers were neither disengaged nor fearfully shying away from perceived injustices. In 2004 Eva Sallis, writing on the transformative power of literature, noted: 'Where there are changes in any country where, on the one hand, people are being hurt and, on the other hand, people ignore or are blind to that hurt, you will find that writers and artists of all kinds are driven to create the works that . . . provoke thought and engagement for readers.'[1] And yet that same year, in the Preface to *Authors Take Sides: Iraq and the Gulf War* (MUP, 2004), Louise Adler wrote: 'It is my melancholy duty to report that in 2004 the idea that writers are society's conscience, making sense of the human condition for the rest of us, is far from universal wisdom.'

It is not only Australian writers who have come under attack for perceived passivity. In March 2007 British journalist Henry Porter, writing in the *Observer* under the headline 'Where is our Orwell, where is our Dickens?', railed against what he saw as the silence of intellectuals afraid to challenge the policies of the Blair government. The country's agenda, complained Porter, was being set by think-tanks and it had reached the stage where lawyers, rather than writers and intellectuals, had 'the most interesting things to say'. He continued: 'Where are the novelists with their indictments of government and society? . . . Where are the dramatists who can barely speak for their anger?' With the exception of David Hare and Harold Pinter, he argued, 'artists have absented themselves from the floor since Labour came into power. We are much worse off for it because we desperately need the moral force of an independent-minded writer training his or her guns on a target.'[2] Earlier, Susan Sontag had painted a picture of American society startlingly similar to Australia. In her polemical essay 'A Few Weeks After', she described a country turning inward in the face of fear. Sontag commented on the resurgence of the American flag and patriotism and of the silencing of any criticism about either the President or the nation, before chillingly noting: 'Self-censorship, the most important and most successful form of censorship, is rampant. Debate is identified with dissent, which is in turn identified with disloyalty.'[3]

Australian readers recognise this strategy by which debate is characterised as dissent and is further dismissed by being labelled 'elitist' or 'unAustralian'. Clive Hamilton's and Sarah Maddison's edited collection, *Silencing Dissent* (Allen & Unwin, 2007) demonstrates powerfully the many ways in which the Howard government, from 1996, sought to stifle political dissent. In the climate of terror brought on by events of 2001, ASIO (the Australian Security Intelligence Organisation) and the federal government tried to convince Australians that we could no longer afford our traditional freedoms. With the introduction of new anti-sedition laws in 2006, we have reached a point where some stories are no longer able to be told. The reporting of certain issues, those deemed to threaten national security, now carries a five-year imprisonment term. As David Marr pointed out in 'His Master's Voice' (*Quarterly Essay* 26, 2007), there is now unprecedented executive control over political communication. A very real concern for the consequences of this kind of control is expressed in Eva Sallis's 'Art in a time of crisis' which opens this collection. Sallis's essay is a rallying call to Australian writers and readers to resist the growing restrictions on their freedom, particularly their freedom of speech. Peter Manning's 'Writing in an "Age of Terror"' is a disturbing piece when read in the context of this closing-down of information. Manning indicates the extent to which the media manipulates its audience to shape agendas that have little to do with truth or justice, before pointing out that 'big-picture issues' require space for reportage and discussion, and that space, he writes, is no longer made available by the mainstream media.

Of course, sometimes the furthering of justice may involve staying silent or suppressing part of the truth, at least until a later date. Frank Brennan's essay offers some potent examples of specific incidents when justice is best served by these strategies. In the broader picture, however, it is the apparent silence or effective acquiescence of the federal opposition in the face of potentially destructive legislation that is disturbing writers and other Australian citizens alike. The introduction of the Crimes Legislation Amendment (National Investigative Powers and Witness Protection) Bill 2006 [2007], which gives the police power not only to enter and search someone's home without their knowledge but also to not tell them for as long as six months afterwards that they have conducted a search, indicates how what were once considered in this country to be basic human rights are being threatened.

For Indigenous Australians that threat has become a reality. On 21 June 2007 Mal Brough, Minister for Families, Community Services and Indigenous Affairs, announced that the federal government would be sending troops into Aboriginal communities across the country as an emergency response to *Ampe Akelyernemane Meke Mekarle 'Little Children are Sacred': The Report of the Northern Territory Board of Inquiry into the Protection of Aboriginal Children from Sexual Abuse*, authored by Pat Anderson and Rex Wild. (In Sydney that same evening it was announced that Waanyi woman Alexis Wright had won the Miles Franklin Award for her huge, complex novel *Carpentaria*, a novel that celebrates the timeless, sustaining power of ancestral stories and storytelling in the face of exploitation and injustice.) Over 600 pages of legislation, which sanctions the requisition of Aboriginal leases and the withholding of social welfare payments to Aboriginal people and which allows the federal government to override the *Racial Discrimination Act 1975*, the *Northern Territory Land Rights Act 1976* and other pieces of welfare legislation, were debated for only nine hours in the House of Representatives. Following that debate, all five Bills were passed in less than one hour. There was no dissenting voice, no dissenting vote. In light of this background, it is imperative we read what three of our leading Indigenous writers, Kim Scott, Anita Heiss and Jane Harrison, have to say about the reclamation of Language, the role of storytelling in affirming and nourishing culture and self-esteem, and the ongoing effects of trauma on Indigenous Australians.

It has been suggested that the invasion of Aboriginal communities was a cynical election ploy intended to bolster support for John Howard's government, like the *Tampa* incident did in the 2001 election. During that incident, crucially, no humanising images of asylum-seekers stranded on the decks of the MV *Tampa* were allowed to be shown to the Australian public. The government knew only too well that it is always easier to dismiss human suffering if that suffering cannot be seen. It is for this reason that asylum-seekers arriving in Australia have been incarcerated behind razor wire in remote desert detention centres that allow no cameras or recording equipment inside. Journalists like David Marr and Marion Wilkinson have insisted on showing readers the personal stories and feelings of asylum-seekers. So too have numerous Australian fiction writers, dramatists and filmmakers. My essay, 'Travelling towards ourselves', explores some of the ways Clara Law's film *Letters to Ali* helps us comprehend and respond to the horror and immorality of incarcerating children. Of particular note is the work done by Sydney PEN, especially Rosie Scott and Tom Keneally as editors of *Another Country*. Through the pages of *Another Country* asylum-seekers are given voice and audience. As readers, we recognise a common humanity with these previously faceless, nameless 'others'. The lives and experiences we discover in those stories are physically, emotionally and psychologically remote from the lives of most Australians. If we are open to them, however, they operate to enlarge and complicate our lives and to help us understand, even just a little, what the reality of detention entails. They engender compassion rather than fear. Rosie Scott discusses the process of compiling *Another Country* and the reception of the work in her essay 'In Praise of Political Fiction'.

Good writing facilitates the opening of borders: of our hearts, our country, our minds. There is never any way of knowing how a particular piece of writing will effect change because it works always on the imagination. Kevin Hart and Ariel Dorfman have each told stories of meeting South American survivors of torture who clung to poetry throughout their ordeals as a means of protecting their sense of self. Dorfman writes of a Chilean woman: 'That was how she had protected her besieged identity, the one thing those jailers could not touch, could not deny her, could not erase: just some words, just some precarious, almost evanescent, words from the past as a defence against what seemed an eternity of pain and humiliation.' Noel Rowe's essay demonstrates through its discussion of the poetry of Eva Johnson, Rosemary Dobson, Judith Wright and Francis Webb how poetry works through images, metaphor, tone and speaking positions to create a relational ethic. Rowe points out that justice, in the way it is so often predicated on loss, participates in elegy. Gail Jones's 'Speaking shadows: Justice and the poetic' meditates on grief and mourning as it weaves its way from a consideration of the 'ethically difficult' poetry of Paul Celan, through the darkness of the Stolen Generations, to a discussion of how personal and national memory (and forgetting) inform the writing of her latest novel, *Sorry*. Jones finishes her piece acknowledging that writing should be unsettling, difficult and uncertain and that it is the reader who is the final repository of an author's words and ideas. Similarly, Katherine Thomson's essay, which outlines the genesis and writing of a number of her award-winning plays and screenplays, celebrates the importance of the audience and sees the theatre as a unique space which allows the audience to 'worry collectively' about the issues they are faced with. In contrast, Adrian Martin's 'Boring humanist bodies' rails against what Martin sees as a lack of daring, imaginative creation in mainstream Australian cinema. Like the other contributors to this collection, Martin wants writing, here filmic writing, to address the 'tough burning issues of Australian reality'. As things currently stand, he feels, the spectator is being short-changed.

In 1973 Australian writer and scholar Dorothy Green delivered a lecture on 'The Place of Literature in Society'. She defined literature as 'any piece of work made of words which gives me pleasure as well as information' and she stressed how important it was for perceptive readers to be part of the conversation writing initiates. 'Literature', she concluded, 'either spoken or written, is humanity thinking aloud – communicating its experience of all that is, holding a great continuous discussion through the ages and across the world.'[4] This collection of essays is designed to contribute to that vital, ongoing conversation about writing and justice that is happening in this country despite the many powerful forces operating to thwart it.

The contributors to this collection include poets, playwrights, fiction and non-fiction writers and a film critic. Each was given the same brief: to write an essay on the theme of writing and justice. Perhaps not surprisingly the essays overlap in places. Taken as a whole, they deal with a cluster of issues that centre around Indigenous rights, asylum-seekers, freedom of speech, accountability and truth in media, unionism, Australian history and the rich, complex relationship between language and justice. Of course, there is no simple answer to the question 'What is justice?', first posed by Plato in his *Republic* and debated by philosophers ever since. There is, however, consensus among a diverse range of thinkers that justice is concerned with maximising the common good; that justice is enacted when the correct relationships between individuals, between groups and between the individual and the state are established and maintained; and that justice strives to ensure equity and fairness. These are the principles on which this collection is based.

The essays collected here are not *just* crafted *words*, they are *words* crafted about *justice*. It is hoped they have the power to move readers and to effect change, whether that be practical change or imaginative change. *Just Words?* is a mix of biographical pieces that explore the imaginative and practical processes of writing and more theoretical essays that seek to analyse how writing models justice. The underlying premise of the collection is that writers are essential to healthy civic discourse, but so too are readers. These essays aim to contribute to a more robust public discussion initiated by the writers and readers of Australia.

Art in a time of crisis

Eva Sallis

In most societies the opinions of writers and artists occupy a special place, being seen as neither private individual opinion nor exactly expert opinion. The freedom to offer these opinions is a test of the freedoms in any society, as is the freedom to express what I would see as destructive and divisive ideas. An often-used metaphor for freedom of speech (with strange and disturbing overtones) is the coal-mine canary in the cage. Its death indicates the presence of an insidious and pervasive threat.

It is notable that those who do communicate through art are also often political dissenters, and silencing them is one of the purposes of controls on freedom of speech in highly controlled societies. Many Iraqis who fled Saddam Hussein's regime were in danger because they were writers, their flight and plight mirrored around the world in countries where people are physically and psychologically abused by the state and where those in power would rather it was not talked about. Writers have a tendency to write about the unspeakable. And that is the source of it. Canaries sing compulsively, and writers write compulsively about what they have seen, thought or imagined. This may not be expert opinion, or private opinion, but it can be a threat to those in power. The demonstrated ability to use one's imagination and to communicate about it is both admired and at times feared, although not often nor by many in Australia.

I was in Moscow in 2006. I arrived the day after writer Anna Politkovskaya was shot point-blank outside her apartment. Anna Politkovskaya wrote passionately and fearlessly about the unspeakable horrors of Chechnya, and was an outspoken critic of government. She was at the Sydney Writers' Festival recently, and was a writer admired the world over for her courage. I gathered from the media in Russia that Politkovskaya was both loved and reviled in Russia, and speculation rages still on whether state, rogue or mafia elements were responsible for the professional-style killing.

Politkovskaya's death made me think about my own writing on refugees and asylum-seekers in Australia, and on the privileges of peace and the rule of law in my country. This is an opinion piece written without fear in what for me personally is a peaceful and safe land. I live in a country in which at this moment I can express my opinions without consequence, no matter the gulf between my views and those of the government of the day. I do not risk arrest in the middle of the night, interrogation and intimidation. I do not put my family at risk, and I am not in danger of blackmail, or from rogue or mafia elements. I certainly do not risk torture, death or exile. The most unpleasant it can get for me is nasty emails and the loss of some friendships. Furthermore, for me as a writer, allegory, humour and other forms of masked criticism are just some of the many choices I have at the moment, rather than the only choice I have, for expressing dissent in art.

Arguably, much literature published in Australia through the 1980s and 1990s was very inward looking. It explored a passionate personal and general interest in the question 'Who are we?'. Just think of all the very successful revisitations of our past: *The Drowner*, *The Sound of One Hand Clapping*, *Mr Darwin's Shooter*, *Remembering Babylon*. Who are we? Just think of all the powerful and revealing lifestyle novels – *Praise*, *Candy* – novels of the Australian city, grunge novels. Who are we? Think of the passion for autobiography, generally and specifically; Aboriginal women's autobiography, a genre in itself.

David Malouf wrote in *A Spirit of Play: The Making of Australian Consciousness* that we begin to belong to a land when that land appears in our works of imagination – when our poetry, literature and art express that land in us and through us. The same is true of peoples. The 1980s and 1990s saw multicultural literature cease as a marginalised sub-genre and a new Australian artistic self emerge and find an uneasy acceptance in the mainstream of literary fiction, often by shock or surprise – think of Christos Tsiolkas's *Loaded*, or the gentler *Looking for Alibrandi*, or the works of Brian Castro and many others.

Through the early part of this century, however, that core question has changed, at least it has for me and I think many other writers. I am starting to seek and respond to art that perhaps has at its core the question 'What are we becoming?'. In some ways this is a much more outward-looking question than 'Who are we?'. It is a question that draws in painful doubts on right and wrong and explores the web of nationhood, culture and belonging.

Why the shift? I believe this is caught up in the relationship between imagination and dissent. Many writers, if they are able to imagine injustices played out in the lives of people, will write about them, and Australia has become steadily more unjust over the past decade. It may seem strange to suggest that current policies, new laws and social changes could generate a new Australian literature, given that Australia is still comparatively peaceful and safe and is a first-world democracy with a highly materialistic, capitalist ethos and a high standard of living. But speaking for myself, a changing Australia has wrought great change on my sensibility – on my aesthetics, let alone my political views. I cannot view Australia complacently, and I cannot ignore the pressure to find a way to write about human cruelties here, past and present.

Authoritarian governments like to control people's capacity to imagine some things. In Australia, which is experiencing a weird and senseless flirtation with authoritarianism, this control of the capacity to imagine is most apparent in the current government's handling of refugees and detention centres. Out of sight and inaccessible, refugees and asylum-seekers were en masse hurt and damaged by us, as well as being actively vilified and demonised by government in the hope that Australians would accept a dehumanised view and not try to imagine what it is like to be them.

From 2000 we have seen the rise of grassroots movements in response to the government's hardline approach to refugees arriving unauthorised. These grassroots movements, like broad shifts in art and literature towards dissent, are a symptom of human rights keeling over in a country and the fading of public imagination and compassion. Yes, they are inspiring, and they point to some terrific qualities in ordinary Australians, but they don't spring up in their hundreds, all on the theme of rights, when a government is taking care to ensure that basic rights of all are protected.

These movements were and are made up of individuals from all walks of life. A very large number of lawyers have been involved from early in the movement: it was only lawyers who really understood the implications of amendments to the *Migration Act*. An overwhelming number of artists and writers also got involved, or even got up and formed these groups.

Artists and writers do not have a monopoly on imagination – far from it. But in any society we do expect them to be among those who have it and use it. Howard's government fears positive public imagination. In one sense it also uses the imaginings that fear generates, but I want to use the term 'public imagination' here specifically for that capacity a community has to imagine the lives of others – in other words, a shared capacity to think and feel with others. I like to use the word 'imagination' rather than the more discredited word 'compassion'.

We are in a time of crisis, even if it is a mini-crisis compared with upheavals in other countries. It has been building incrementally since 1996, cranked up with great speed since 2001. Our new anti-terror legislation was rushed though just over a year ago as though Australia was under imminent threat and a patched-up grab bag of laws was needed immediately. This was just a stunt, we now know, but as a result we have in force some poisonous legislation that, despite influential calls for amendment, is barely changed. Under this new legislation, Australians can be detained without charge, and can be tried without ever knowing the evidence being used against them.

This legislation reactivates and expands archaic sedition laws, making clear that this government fears the influence of the written and spoken word. Don't phrases like 'sedition' and 'detention without charge' sound strange to your ears? Don't they sound a dull warning note?

Under new sedition laws I theoretically have to watch what I say in public speeches and in my fiction. For some of it I have been provided with a defence. Were I to stand up and say that reductionist good and evil policy making and waging unjust wars creates terrorists far more effectively than any individual's good opinion of Usama Bin Laden ever could, then I would have to defend myself by showing somehow that such criticism and encouragement of Australia's 'enemies' is made in 'good faith', whatever that means exactly. But the legislation is not necessarily linked to terrorism. Any kind of support for 'enemies' is proscribed. There is no real defence of good faith, it seems, for fiction or the arts generally. The effect of any such legislation is achieved in the first instance though intimidation. Would I find a publisher for 'Aftermath', an essay I wrote for a book called *Why the War Was Wrong*, now such legislation is in force? Would the publisher have commissioned it? If so-called 'competent authorities' believe that John Pilger's work is seditious, or encourages acts of violence, then the government has the power to arrest and hold him without charge for two weeks in weird bad-thriller secrecy that is defined and protected by legislation. Until Pilger is defending himself in a court, he would not be allowed the help of a lawyer, since that is the purpose of secret questioning. And then he could get up to seven years in prison.

Furthermore, why would anyone assume that secret questioning without legal advice and without rights of any kind (questioning that Pilger, were he subjected to it, would not even be allowed to mention to his family) would be civilised and reflect so-called Australian values of a fair go, mateship and easy-going flexibility or commonsense? Such questioning would involve extremes of bullying and intimidation when its purpose was to shut someone up, and would involve torture when its purpose was to extract information. That is what secrecy is for. There is no country in the world that I can think of, past or present, that uses secrecy honourably and with respect for people's rights. If you don't believe me that this is possible here and now, do some research on what took place in Woomera and Curtin detention centres before their secrecy was partly eroded. That is us, this government, here and now.

Some writers might be prepared to put up with this, especially if self-employed. To be outspoken also seems to me to be part of our job as writers. Some might find it hard to shut up. I have faith that John Pilger will always speak out. We would have to weigh up the effect on our families, the level of personal intimidation. We are, after all, in peaceful, safe Australia, where the rule of law rarely breaks out in boils. We are not in Russia – we risk far less than Anna Politkovskaya did. But what of journalists in Australia? Journalists whose job it is to research and tell a story so that people can imagine a complex rather than a pre-packaged world and imagine what it is like for someone the government would rather they did not think about? How many journalists will be able to risk the costs of a trial and the inconvenience to their already partisan employers? What will Australian society be like when the only story you ever see or hear in the media is the one the government of the day would like you to imagine?

We are now not too far away from the notion of exiled writers. We are already banning books. Frank Moorhouse's important essay 'The Writer in a Time of Terror'[1] outlines all the significant pointers to the erosion of rights in Australia and the current shaky and unhealthy state of freedom of speech. It makes for sober reading. The temptation to ban books is high when books believed to be dangerous are published, but the temptation to ban books for the political effect of deeming them dangerous on relatively slim evidence is perhaps even higher. It is effective in scaring people and especially publishing companies into compliance, encouraging self-censorship, and it is effective in sustaining levels of fear in the public mind. In the past twelve months we have begun banning books for the first time since the early 1970s.

If Australians Against Racism, just one of the many small grassroots movements, or I, in my capacity as its president, made an outspoken statement against the vilification of Muslims here and abroad, against the war, and against our government's policy on terrorism, then, as I understand it, the attorney-general would have the power to ban the organisation. Of course he wouldn't – it is very hard from a commonsense view to see Australians Against Racism as having anything to do with terrorism – but what if, down the track, an attorney-general would like to? What if ideas we hold dear, ideas of multiculturalism, pluralism and public imagination, are sufficiently derided that banning an organisation like Australians Against Racism becomes acceptable in the eyes of the electorate? Under this legislation there is no defence. Will this be the beginning of the end of any NGO's political role? Will this eventually be the end of Human Rights Watch reports that have Australian researchers, the end of Amnesty International membership for Australian citizens and residents?

We are creating the preconditions also for a secret police. Of course it is nonsense to suggest that the Australian government now or in the future would like to have a secret police at its disposal. But why create the preconditions that could sustain such a force? Why lean towards extrajudicial justice? Where will this take us? Should we ignore the possibility that we might be creating the preconditions for atrocity? We have a group in society almost sufficiently feared and dehumanised; a legislature that is more and more powerless to intervene; a populace that is increasingly living in fear, and accepting the curtailment of rights and freedoms for the sake of security; freedom of speech threatened; and innocence until proven guilty overturned. Shouldn't we all be shouting, loudly, now, before it is too late?

Realistically, at first little will happen. Australia lives in complacent peace and prosperity, and at the very least the collective momentum of all our expectations of freedom and preservation of our way of life will carry us through quite significant erosions of that freedom. Fringe-dwellers in our society will be hit hardest as their unsafe and uncertain Australia is increasingly disregarded. I am thinking of Aboriginal Australians and any other marginalised groups that do not get to share mainstream ease, mainstream safety, mainstream protection at law. The anti-terror legislation has problems in principle and to principled people, but a certain guilty commonsense suggests that the government will use this legislation to chase down incautious sheikhs they disagree with and to harass Muslim youth, and that the arts are really safe to go on as they have for the past few decades. We guess that political protest will be a little more difficult in public, and that getting political work published will also be harder, but no one really expects to be detained for questioning or charged with sedition. We guess that the application of such laws will be political and discretionary. In other words, put bluntly, we all know that any application of these laws will at first be racist. And when I am seditious, which I suspect will be often, I will have the unpleasant knowledge that I will be speaking because the government chooses to allow it, not because I have a right to.

Just over a year ago, when the anti-terror laws were only a scary proposal, I wanted to get an idea of the more indirect effects this legislation might have on the arts and on freedom of speech. I rang a literary agent I know well to ask her views, and found her deeply disturbed by the proposed laws and their implications. She was adamant that she would never reject a novel because of potentially seditious content. And, until publishers get shaky, she would seek publication for it in Australia. She was refreshingly feisty too. She said that we should all have in place codes by which we can let people know that we have been detained without actually saying it.

I rang and asked one of Australia's smaller publishers what his views were. He said that he thought publishers would not be on the frontline in the way that journalists might be. He suggested that, as a publisher and a citizen, he found these laws objectionable. But as we discussed it, he said thoughtfully that even the costs of seeking legal advice on a particular book might be off-putting to some publishers, let alone getting advice that they were exposed to a potential lawsuit. He said something about book publishing being a clearing house for ideas and then trailed off. He sounded depressed.

I rang one of the bigger publishers and spoke to a commissioning editor. She was quite fierce about her company's commitment to Australia's cultural and intellectual life. She said, 'Put it this way – let's see how many seditious books we can get out in the next twelve months.' She also thought that good books would come out of this, that it might be a wake-up call to many sleeping thinkers in the country. She sounded as though her company would be prepared at least for a while to pit itself against the government on this one. But if litigation became a real possibility, she said that the company would have to help authors to find less overt ways of communicating important ideas.

I asked a journalist. She said there was consternation among her colleagues, but that the spirit on the floor was that journalists must keep reporting the truth and the facts regardless; there was even a feeling, among younger journalists, that these were exciting times, a challenge to meet. She believed too that the laws would not affect people much at first, but that journalists would be affected before other writers or private individuals. She wondered what would happen the first time the Australian Federal Police demanded a journalist reveal a source under the new laws, and how many journalists would go to prison. Then we got talking about the highly seditious play she is writing on the side.

Since then, in 2006 alone (most of these are from Frank Moorhouse's article), the attorney-general took over the Classification and Review Boards from the Office of Film and Literature Classification in order to secure the banning of eight books which had not been banned through all the usual processes; the staging of a political performance that satirised John Howard was prevented by police at a public protest, with police claiming they were enforcing sedition laws; a Melbourne public literary event expressly forbade the reading of poems with political content; and a creative website presenting an extended ironic apology by John Howard was shut down. Two books of the eight were banned, finally, in July 2006; the attorney-general proposed tougher laws in order to secure the banning of the remaining six books; and, of course, terror suspects and their families are gagged by the laws and cannot even talk about rumours of degrading treatment in Australian prisons. What does this show? It shows a rapid creep of the misuse and abuse of powers, and the more gradual seepage of self-censorship.

There is, rightly, dismay among writers, artists and arts industries, just as there was dismay among lawyers, barristers and judges in 1999 when changes to legislation began to remove the basic principle of universal human rights and equality before the law. The anti-terror legislation has thrown away the civil society we once had, a society in which injustice could be properly debated and questioned. Once a book a government really dislikes is published and the first publisher is charged, self-censorship will take hold and mainstream publishing of dissenting voices will cease. I, like Frank Moorhouse, see the threat from extremism as real, and think an attack on Australian soil is inevitable. But trying to control what people think, say or write has never been the answer. What will we do after the first attack on Australian soil? The government of that sad day has been empowered by this vague legislation to do a great deal to any slightly dissenting individual it cares to target, and we can expect draconian legislation to come into force, given that we let this one through without true outcry. The racism and culture hatred won't go away – but we will have more and more difficulty talking about it, or exposing the abuses that necessarily come along with it.

It is not self-interest that makes writers defend freedom of speech at the first sign of its serious curtailment. Freedom of speech is the key freedom; it is the means by which all other breaches of individual rights and abuses of power are made manifest and fought over. Freedom of speech is the test of a free society, the test that a society sees itself capable of full and open debate and full exposure to facts. Russia does not yet have such a society, although it is struggling towards having one, if Putin is to be believed. Australia recently had such a society. Freedom of speech is the marker of a social and intellectual fabric that is diverse enough and strong enough to cope with divisive and destructive opinions of individuals or groups. Everyone should be very worried about the long-term survival of basic rights in a society when a government begins to seek secrecy and to control what one can know and say about its actions. Everyone should leap up and dissent at the first sign that the government might like the power to silence individual opinion and to muzzle the media.

So, what is the role of art, of literature, in a time of crisis, even if it is the subtle crisis that is happening almost invisibly in Australia?

For a while longer, we will get published, we will get exhibited, we will get grants for politically charged work, and we will get audiences. The time is coming when we may have to use allegory, satire, humour and metaphor, and stage illegal performances. But right now, the time is here for artists, musicians, writers, filmmakers and dramaturges to express what we are becoming. Art in a time of crisis is about invoking the capacity to think and feel beyond ourselves, and to imagine the lives of others. Art is about keeping alive some part of the public imagination.

This has become threatening. Subtly or unsubtly we are being asked to cease to imagine some human beings. They are becoming ciphers, symbols, evil forces, evil hordes, Dark Lords, allegedly functioning beyond ordinary human motivation, beyond morality, beyond ordinary comprehension. We are being told now that it is wrong to even try to imagine them, in case this encourages them. We all know who they are: terrorists, suicide bombers, Islamists, Usama bin Laden, insurgents, Mullah Omar, al-Zarqawi, Amrozi, Jema'a Islamiya. They have Islam and violence in common. We don't agree with capital punishment, but can make an exception for these ciphers. We don't agree with extrajudicial killing, unless it is Saddam Hussein and his sons and grandson. We don't condone torture of human beings, but turn a blind eye to it if it is a terrorist. Whatever form dehumanisation takes, I think art must resist it, speak against the current; it must find the stories, metaphors and images that will shock us with ourselves and will take us, at least for a moment, beyond this fearful fantasy. Art is powerless to stop us going to war. But it can bear witness. It is the job of art to bear witness.

The curtailment of freedom of speech and the control of the media is the curtailment of public imagination. More and more Australians will cease to recognise some Australians as human. Once exiled from our imagination, what are young Arab Australians to become? If we continue to ratchet up the alienation young Arab and Muslim Australians feel, what will be the consequences? Where will they go to find themselves as Australians, their role in Australian history? Exile from the common imagination is the most terrible thing ever to happen to a group of human beings and has irreparable consequences. We should know that from history.

Artists must use all the imagination they have to wake people from this poisonous and tragic fantasy. We are far enough gone that such awakening is deeply painful.

Australia is unreconciled, at war with ourselves, suspicious of all and willing our own blindness, our own destruction. *Who are we? What are we doing? What are we becoming?* These core questions will drive thinkers, artists and writers for a long time to come. And yet most of us are still safe in our houses. How could we throw away so much before we even had to live and die as Anna did?

Writing in an 'Age of Terror'

Peter Manning

'Justice' derives from the Latin word for 'right'. And 'right' has a moral quality about it or, at the very least, a suggestion of 'fairness'. I am not a moral philosopher, but I can recognise the deep roots of moral judgments that have infused my life for as long as I can remember; a Catholic education with the Christian Brothers saw to that. Searching for what was 'right', distinguishing it from what was 'wrong', was a common pursuit at school, echoed at Sunday Mass. Luckily, my family was not so determined to continue the pursuit. My mother took a more relaxed, amused view of human behaviour. She had many stories both from the Second World War and from migrants she had met in Australia who had gone through massive refugee trauma. Moral judgments did not count high on her list. My father just wanted me to get a good education. While his family had been of Irish Catholic background, he was sent off to Grafton High School in the 1920s, and he infused me with a set of secular values that were mainly about being Australian, enjoying sport and believing in the 'fair go' for all and support for the underdog. That ended up with him voting for Robert Gordon Menzies, which I didn't understand, but the rest of my family was solidly Labor.

So it was surprising for me when I got to Sydney University to run into a Catholic chaplain, Fr Ted Kennedy, who was resolutely against 'judgmentalism'. My impression from school was that the Church was all about rushing to judgment. Certainly my memory of the English teacher who did a rendition from the blackboard of what the Russian Communists would do to Catholics in Hungary – he proceeded to pull out his tongue in a gymnastic display beside his desk – was that he made many judgments about 'evil', 'right' and 'wrong' and left us in no doubt about who to back and who not. I was so terrified and outraged at the impending doom of my co-religionists that I went home and penned a letter to the Sydney *Daily Telegraph* condemning Communists, adding my pre-teenage age. The letter got in – my first foray into journalism. I was proud at doing my bit to hold back the evil tide, and especially proud to see my name in print.

By the time I arrived at Sydney University I was chock-a-block with moral judgments. The tide of Communism was even closer: China, Vietnam, Malaya. I enrolled in the Democratic Labor Party Club, which seemed to have the advantage of both being Labor and fighting Communism. Within weeks, a new, charismatic, Catholic American President, John F. Kennedy, was trying to save the world from Communism by halting the installation of Russian missiles in Cuba. The half-defunct DLP Club was called to action – by me! Not being a member of any political party, I got some mates from Catholic schools to join me and we waged a war of attrition – barely months into my fresher year – against the intellectuals supporting Khrushchev. I remember making a particular fool of myself in the august and ancient History Room just off the old quadrangle of the university. I railed from the podium at the audience, only to be interrupted by a Senior Lecturer in American History who appeared to know more than me. I listened to his interjection with grudging politeness. When he sat down, to howls of derision from my supporters but solid clapping from most of the audience, I was a little miffed.

It took a couple of years for it to dawn on me that I might be barking up the wrong tree. A close friend from school did me the service of tapping me on the shoulder in my second year at university about my penchant for 'rushing to judgment'. In particular, he complicated my worldview by asking me to read other books about Vietnam than the ones I had chosen according to my ideology. He had clearly been a bit more sceptical of the official version of events acquired at school. And, as a budding historian, he had taken on board rigorous historical method in his thinking.

But it was Ted Kennedy, the priest, who was most fierce about the rush to moral judgment. He was seriously concerned about his own religion's track record with the Inquisition, with Galileo and with Charles Darwin. But more deeply, he was concerned with 'openness' to new experiences, to people and to difference. He felt the Catholic Church had been so sure of itself in the past few centuries that it had become encrusted with doctrine, oblivious to the poor and closed to new thinking in science, the arts and philosophy. And he was in tune with a new spirit that expressed itself in Pope John XXIII's Second Vatican Council. He felt like fresh air to me. I felt I had made a goose of myself. I hope I learned some lessons.

Where does this sense of moral righteousness come from? On a personal level, I spent some time in later years trying to root it out of my consciousness, having been imbued so young with all the certainties. On a more broad level, it is a particularly important question in this 'age of terror', this age of fundamentalism: Hindu fundamentalism, Christian fundamentalism, Jewish fundamentalism and, of course, Muslim fundamentalism. For fundamentalism is not only a spring-cleaning of distractions, false idols and dangerous ideas, it is also a drive to regain the eternal essentials. What begins as a spring-clean ends up as endless distinctions about who is inside the tent and who is outside. Toleration of doubt, uncertainty, nuance, subjectivity, interpretation, development and, finally, difference becomes impossible.

John Howard's reign in government has been marked by a political fundamentalism that constantly wants to draw the line between those who are 'true Australians' and those who are not. It followed a purge within his own party of who was a 'true Liberal' and who was not. And it was followed by a continual defining of the line in foreign policy about who was 'us' and who was 'them'. The Americans under neo-conservative George Bush and the

Israelis under former war criminal Ariel Sharon were 'us', the Arabs and the Muslims were 'them'. 'We' in 'the West' would support 'our' people in Iraq and Israel/Palestine. This was whether they wanted us to be involved or not and whether, too, the majority of Australians wanted to be in Iraq or not. 'Us' was an ideological, not a statistical, reality.

So another question follows on from the question of moral righteousness and its roots. It is this: When do we define someone as different? Further questions follow: Why is there such a modern need to see difference as threatening rather than enhancing? What fear drives us backwards into boundaries? What are the mechanisms at work that say we cannot handle this or that amount of difference? These concepts, of course, go to the heart of the debate about multiculturalism in Australia and elsewhere. Some see the breakdown of multiculturalism leading, in a global sense, to the alleged 'clash of civilisations'. These are social anthropological questions of a high order. I suspect we won't know the answers to these questions about our times until it is too late. The answers will be useful as historical constructs but not as current moral or political data. We can only hint at some patterns that bring together questions of morality, justice, difference and peace – and the role of writers, writing and the media.

Between the lines

There's a game that the media plays with its publics. It goes like this: we'll pretend to be a document of record with separate areas for opinion but both we and our audience know not only the slant of this enterprise but that every element is riven with subjectivity. No one 'believes' in their newspaper, news broadcast or even shock-jock any more. Media credibility is at an all-time low. High-school students entertain themselves and learn how to analyse manipulative media product with texts like *Frontline* or *Media Watch*. The twin current affairs programs, *A Current Affair* (Nine Network) and *Today Tonight* (Seven), compete for the lowest ground, performing the role of the circus from medieval days. Populist newspapers fill front pages with editorial screamers that express moral judgments on the news of the day. Lifestyle journalism dominates over investigative journalism: where can you find the best latte/haircut/film/nightclub rather than uncovering the workings of the power elite. Such reporting is made worse by the impact of satellites and the flood of digital communication at the expense of content, connecting everyone to everyone. You can construct your own digital world on a stream of technologies. But what do you want them to say? Or what do you want to say to them?

In this environment it is not what is said in the text so much as what is not said. It is the audience's *understanding* of what was said that matters. It is the 'dog whistle' between the lines. And in this space all things are possible. Again, John Howard is the master of the art. If Paul Keating had the nation attuned to his one-liners, Howard has the nation attuned to his symbolic message. That message is carefully crafted about difference: whether you are 'on board' the good ship Australia or not, whether you are a winner or a loser, whether you are reasonable or unreasonable, whether you are living in the past or are a modern kind of person, whether you are an ordinary Aussie or a presumptuous git. When Howard, Carr, Costello and Ruddock tell Muslims they don't like that they can 'shape up or ship out', the 'dog whistle' message is that these Muslims are barely Australian and are able to be exported at the drop of a hat. The truth is, most Muslims in Australia were born here, are as Australian as the rest of us and will remain living where they are. They are part of our community, not aliens.

The dog whistle is so-called because it recalls the sheep farmer who can direct his dog to turn the sheep in any direction depending on his whistle. In this analogy, farmer Howard whistles the dog (through the media) and the sheep follow (us). This idea merely mimics Michel Foucault, Stuart Hall, Raymond Williams and other media theorists. It advances the argument about all media statements being subjectively received: from the earliest 'gatekeeper' studies in the United States – showing how many times any one idea changes as it goes through the daily news process – to the latest work of Pierre Bourdieu (see, for example, *On Television*, published by Pluto Press in 1998). But it has a special importance in the twenty-first century as habits of media consumption become ever more ephemeral, discontinuous and sensuous. Determining the symbolic message – the real message – of the media 'text' has never been more important.

Writing about justice, in any form, therefore must take into account not only the forms of media and the characteristics of their special platforms and attractions but also the way in which they are received and regarded. It is difficult to believe that a 6.30 pm commercial 'current affairs' program is taken as anything other than circus comedy, whereas a rock video (downloaded to a mobile) from the latest hip-hop group may be taken extremely seriously. The rock video may carry the dog whistle message more effectively than a program held in little regard.

Scepticism and justification

When I was head of News and Current Affairs at ABC Television, I used to tell some groups of journalists that they should never forget that their audiences were more intelligent than they were. It was a deliberately unsettling remark. In my experience I have found that journalists assume not only that they know a lot about a lot of things but also that they are well ahead on most things, barring specialist knowledge in, say, brain surgery. Older reporters or presenters in the current affairs genre especially can come to feel they've dug into most subjects with some depth and are merely recycling their encyclopaedic knowledge. In making such a statement I was playing on a well-known disregard that those in the industry know commercial current affairs producers have for their audiences. One executive producer at *60 Minutes* used to refer to his audience as 'string bags' – merely dumb consumers who could be manipulated by demographic story by story.

But there was an important underlying point to the remark. Any piece of script had to take the audience through the narrative assuming every viewer had to be *convinced* of the various propositions being advanced. An investigative program like *Four Corners*, for instance, not only had to announce its hypothesis up front but then had to proceed to convince the viewer, through tangible pieces of evidence, of the truth of the conclusion. On the way, it had to confront the scepticism of thousands of university-educated professionals who often began with the proposition that all journalists were shonky. Add to that the natural sympathy of Australians for 'the underdog' (the accused) and the task of each reporter to convince the viewer that the only explanation for the behaviour under review was the one the reporter proposed. So the script had to be a process of elimination, allowing the accused to put his/her view at every stage (in as comprehensive a way as he/she would want for themselves) and yet showing that the conclusion reached by the program was justifiable on the evidence.

The scepticism of the audience was built not only on the endless accounts of journalists rorting evidence, getting it wrong or behaving like clowns. It was also built on the innate idea that people, institutions and even politicians are innocent until proven guilty. Finally, only in exceptional cases would ordinary men and women allow institutions like the media the privilege of making judgments about the guilt or innocence of even the most transparent scoundrels. Investigative programs like *Four Corners* might have earned that exceptional status because it had stuck by the rules of evidence so often and had treated its audience with care and respect over fifty years of reporting. Australians' scepticism towards crusading journalism was held in abeyance.

Populism and justice

But it is not just 'serious' media, 'serious' writing and 'serious' publishing that enable issues of morality, justice and fairness to be addressed. Pollsters say that when they are doing the ratings for television executives they have to discount the viewers who feel they 'should' be watching the ABC or SBS and can't quite bring themselves to admit to a stranger they've been watching *Oprah*, *Judge Judy* or, god forbid, *Big Brother* instead of a wildlife documentary on the ABC. There is a certain snobbishness about populist media even among those who use it on a daily basis.

Yet the differences are not so great. All media sensationalise – it is essential to the form. All media are attracted to the institutions of power – that's where the stories are. All media suffer from discontinuous narratives – they are based on daily 'peak' events. All media are corporatised into world news-gathering networks – that's why a flood in Florida gets big coverage but another one in Guatemala gets none. And all media work on myths – that is why individual human stories are presented as the 'deserving poor', the 'lazy dole bludger', the 'rugged individualist', the 'little battler' and so on week after week.

This point is made by the Palestinian American literary scholar Edward Said in his seminal works, *Orientalism* (1978), *Culture and Imperialism* (1993) and *Covering Islam* (1991). In reviewing the coverage of the 1979 Iranian Revolution in newspapers and talk shows in the United States, Said shows how the 'quality' newspapers like the *New York Times* were as culpable as any in regards to racist and discriminatory imagery of the Ayatollah Khomeini and the students who overthrew the regime of the Shah Pahlavi. He locates their coverage within the broad band of 'orientalist' attitudes towards Arabs and towards Muslims: these people, *by nature*, are devious, untrustworthy, tricky, pre-modern, violent and emotional. This is by contrast with the rational, honest, modern, civilised people of 'the West'. In *Orientalism* Said is at pains to show how old this East–West distinction is, how it has invaded Western thinking for a millennium or more and how it has been institutionalised in universities, foreign affairs departments and the media for centuries. We Westerners are conditioned to see the Arab and the Muslim in mythical terms, not on a case-by-case basis, as we would most people. Stereotypes are allowed to enter both 'quality' and populist media in a way which would never be allowed for black, Jewish or Asian people any longer.

Populist media have the advantage not only of telling the story in more compact form – a considerable attraction when literary attention spans are shortening by the year – but of having bigger audiences. There is a certain democratic notion that says that if 80 per cent of Australians watch commercial channels and only 20 per cent watch the ABC, or equivalent figures in print and radio, then the highly educated, literate middle class that constitutes this rich nation has voted with its feet about what it wants to see, read and hear. This is not an argument for closing the ABC, but for acknowledging that those interested in justice need to stay in touch with the vast majority, not the small minority, and address their concerns. To not do so is to adopt an old English notion that only people who belong to a certain 'class' understand what is good for them. As the media continues to get more democratic, those believing in such an elitist class notion will be voices in the wilderness.

Honesty, not propaganda

Paul Lyneham, the Canberra correspondent for a whole range of ABC and Channel Nine programs, and a friend, once told me that his guiding light in journalism was George Orwell. I told him Orwell was mine, too. I think it's true for a lot of my generation. We admired Orwell mostly because of his private letters and correspondence, published in two volumes so many years ago. They show a man of ruthless honesty: ruthless on his own wayward dalliances with the Left and the Right, ruthless on his editors to let him tell the truth of what he sees, and ruthlessly sceptical of the wars fought in service of the Big Ideas. In *Homage to Catalonia* (1938), a lot of his doubts about the Spanish Civil War and the role of the fascist and communist backers of the two sides surface. The moment when he sees the neck of an enemy soldier in his gunsights is particularly moving.

But what we've admired about Orwell was his willingness to change when the facts didn't seem to fit with his picture of the world. Ironically, I was introduced to Orwell by Dr Frank Knopfelmacher, a psychology lecturer and intellectual leader of the right-wing putsch at Melbourne University, when I was in the DLP Club at Sydney University. It was Orwell who helped me move to the Left over Vietnam and to acknowledge the force of nationalism in the Vietnamese people's struggle to rid themselves of both the French and the Americans. To me, Orwell was, and has continued to be, the writer par excellence who remains honest to himself regardless of the propaganda value for the cause he might be serving.

I was reminded of Orwell when Chris Masters and I were doing a film for *Four Corners* about the chemical Agent Orange. Our thesis was that if

Australian Vietnam veterans were suffering from exposure to Agent Orange, then surely the hundreds of thousands of ordinary Vietnamese we dropped it on must also be affected. After the trip to various Vietnamese hospitals, experts and fields, we returned to Australia to interview a Melbourne microbiologist who said there was no causal connection yet established between the chemical and the effects. There was a circumstantial connection, but no scientific one. He knocked our central thesis clear out of the water.

I remember us sitting in the camera car discussing what we would do. Aware of the possible waste of public money, I was re-jigging the film for a different edit. I have to say Chris was more Orwellian than me, insisting we drop our thesis and construct a different film. He was right, of course, but it took me a little time to come to that Orwellian moment of truth. In the end, we re-edited the film from material we had shot to tell a different story, acknowledging the scientist's torpedo!

A sense of understanding

In talking about justice, the media and publishing cannot take a big-picture approach to any given problem. The American sociologist C. Wright Mills, in *The Power Elite* (1956), wrote of the inability of the media, intellectuals and writers to give a sense of understanding of the forces that shape people's lives and how they might get some sense of history and context. Fifty years later, his words hold even more weight.

There are few, if any, ways in which ordinary people can build a broad picture of how one news report fits into a wider picture and in turn how that picture fits within a history and a geographic context. Thailand may be mentioned in today's news for rebel riots in the south of the country but not mentioned again for a month until a monk is found corrupt in Chiang Mai. Apart from the exotic, what does this mean? How can the roots of the struggle for separatism in the south or the declining fortunes of the monks in Thailand be told? This is not an ethereal matter. It becomes more real if Australian young men are asked to fight against 'Muslim terrorists' in the south.

It also becomes more real if the forces that are shaping Australians' lives are due to impact on them soon. Take climate change. It would be interesting to conduct a study of the reporting of the scientists' warnings over the last fifteen years in the Australian media. Apart from Robyn Williams, on ABC Radio National's excellent *The Science Show*, how have ordinary Australians, including the 80 per cent who don't watch or listen to the ABC or SBS, come to know of the dangers facing them? In 2007 it is the talk of the nation and may well influence the upcoming federal election. But the truth is the dire warnings have been there for a decade or more. While most of the world signed up to Kyoto and our federal government teamed up with George Bush to ignore it, what were our media doing to alert Australians to the massive changes to their daily lives that were coming their way? I suspect a decent longitudinal study would show that the media has largely reported the issue only when it has arisen as a political issue between the two sides in Canberra. It has had no means of reporting 'the big picture', of giving Australians understanding. And bar a few books from a couple of scientists, neither has our publishing industry. The 'why wasn't I told' question many Australians might now ask of politicians could be equally directed at the media and publishing houses. The same applies to the decline of manufacturing in Australia. Precious few of our companies do the kind of imaginative work you see from entrepreneurs in countries in Europe of equivalent size without mineral resources: Holland, Spain or Sweden. Why is our corporate sector so uncompetitive internationally unless it is digging up something from the ground?

The state of our soils in the country is yet another example. The overuse of superphosphate and the use of intensive farming, plus now global warming, are destroying the soils of rural Australia. How has this destruction been reported over the last thirty years? Apart from scientific reports in the farmers' newspaper *The Land* and occasional crisis reports from the CSIRO and the Australian Conservation Foundation, this 100-year-old crisis in the making has been allowed to creep up on the average urban Australian until it is too late. Suddenly, anything involving wheat will be costing double. The nature of 'the bush' will have changed, soils will be blowing away and Australians will be ever more a nation living on the fringes of the continent.

'Big picture' issues require a space in our culture that gives ordinary Australians a sense of understanding about where their country is going. Between the academic expertise of research institutions, like the universities and CSIRO, and the increasingly fragmented and digitised media, there has to be a 'community common' where popular conversation about such issues can be debated, analysed and discussed. The gap between reportage and specialist knowledge is wide and increasing. Writers need a space to fill this gap and need to be prepared to think in wider terms.

No media help

For the past six years I have been conducting my own academic research on the media discourse about racism. Specifically, that research has concentrated on how various media report Arabs and Muslims. The surprising prevalence of ancient notions of who these 'different' people are – including Dante finding Mohammed at the bottom of one of his circles in Hell! – appears long before 11 September 2001 and is not explained by that one event. Non-Indigenous Australians have a deep racism about the first Australians. The racism directed towards Arabs and Muslims is distinct from but is related to the race panics about Chinese, Germans, Japanese, Italians, Greeks and Vietnamese. It seems to have dug in deep. The 'melting pot' theory, which posits that every ethnic group will melt into the larger community in time, is not working for them and it bedevils our understanding of important foreign policy issues like Iraq and Israel/Palestine.

My research has clearly had a social justice edge to it and has been used in various quarters to enhance understanding of religious, multicultural and civil society issues. But one aspect of the research is intriguing and deserves further investigation. It is the close parallel between the media narrative on Arabs and Muslims and the state and federal governments' narratives on the same people. I would have thought, as a working journalist, media executive, academic and writer, that the two might have been further apart. Media workers like to think they do not ape the government line. They appear to treasure their independence, regarding it as a cornerstone of democratic society.

But what my work suggests is that the two spheres, government and media, operate far more in tandem, working off each other in complex and interesting ways but not ending up very far from one another. Indeed, sections of the media seem on some occasions to pick up the government ball (state or federal) and simply run with it. This could be caused by a whole series of factors: how the media operates in 'an age of terror/war', the influence of the public relations industry, the growing influence of shock-jock commentators, the impact of the anti-terrorism laws on reporting, the increasing power of pro-government proprietors over their staff, the increased hiring of journalists within government departments and ministers' offices, the dwindling time given to reporters within corporations to check out their own stories, or simply lazy journalism. Whatever the reason, my research suggests that the idea of the two 'estates' at a healthy distance from each other is a convenient myth. It is not quite 'state media' we have on these issues, but it is unhealthily close.

The media has clearly become an even more conservative institution, reflecting the dominant forces of our conservative times. Justice issues are not to be seen. In attempting to champion them, writers, intellectuals, media workers and others will have to forge their own path – even their own media – to create a space for different issues and for different voices. This is even more so following the current federal government's demolition of legal restrictions on foreign ownership of Australian media and cross-media ownership by the current media owners.

Writers and responsibility

Some may think, therefore, that in recognising the need for writers to inform the public of serious 'big picture' issues concerned with justice and social equity, while simultaneously acknowledging the difficulties in covering such issues in the mainstream media, that there is a need to advocate the duty for creative writers, who operate beyond the realm of public media, to step into that gap, to write about justice, to make political issues more honest and more fair. But I would argue that the words 'writer' and 'responsibility' have no relation. In my view, no artist can be loaded with some responsibility to address questions of social justice. I take the neo-Marxist view that we are all artists just as we are all equal in skills across the board. I regard teachers as deserving of the pay of surgeons and applaud the Soviet system of re-ordering pay scales across the board according to social needs. But I do not agree with the Soviet notion of artists serving the state. Did artists have a responsibility to speak up about the Holocaust? Do they have a responsibility to speak up about the ethnic cleansing crimes in Rwanda, Bosnia and the deliberate starvation of today's Palestinians? No.

Only when artists are moved to speak will they speak with truth. While everyone may be an artist, there is a difference between a Shostakovich and a Sydney garage band. As Elizabeth Wilson details in her excellent biography of Shostakovich (*Shostakovitch: A Life Remembered*, 1994), the Soviet state, like Russian regimes before it, ferried Shostakovich away from the fighting front once he had done his famous mid-winter symphony confronting the invading Germans. Mother Russia, even under Stalin, could not afford to lose such precious talent. There is, of course, much debate about whether and how Shostakovich compromised himself in cooperating with the regime in his endeavour to be 'responsible' to The People. But there is consensus that his best work is freely composed and inspired without encumbrances.

No writer will, as Edward Said says, 'speak truth to power' because he or she has to. No 'should' can sit on the shoulder of Australian writers to address political issues. No writer can be reliably hitched to the coat-tails of a political party or cause.

Organic writing

Such critical judgments are fine-line judgments. The best writing is ground-up, from the bowels of the earth. I have a particular interest in racism.

David Malouf seems to me to embody the kind of writing that begins as inspiration and yet explores territory that resonates with the problems Australia faces. His prose is a long, long way from talking about John Howard. But it addresses 'mateship', suburban Australia, sexual relationships, the bush, Australian identity and, above all, the black–white divide. How white Australians live in a black land is a constant theme of his writing. His suggestion of how white Australians 'see' their country through spectres of blackness is so imaginative it astounds me. And it resonates with my history. My aunt told me that my great-grandfather James, an Irish émigré, once worked on the Clarence River boats as they plied their way from Yamba, on the coast, up to Grafton. He was asked to take some poisoned flour downriver to be used on the Aborigines. He refused. Wiping out the first Australians was against his conscience. This would have been around the 1870–80s.

Even today there is a marked difference between the attitude of country people to Aboriginal people and the attitude of white Australians in the city to Aboriginal people. In the country, the feelings of whites seem to me to be visceral. In the city, it ranges from derision to paternalism to genuine friendship and sympathy. In the country, the whites seem to be saying: 'you wankers have no idea what we have to put up with'. In the city, they seem to be saying: 'we are trying to come to terms with what's happened in our history'. But the history of dispossession is far closer for country people than it is for those in the capital cities. It is less than 100 years in some places in Western Australia. The poisonings, the rapes, the brutality, the dispossession is just generations away, on both sides. Malouf catches these tensions and guilt in a welter of country-town experiences.

What makes Malouf special is his *lack of politics*. He is not out to prove a point. He is interested in justice, but that justice comes from what I would call 'organic writing'. By that I mean writing that arises organically from the writer's soul, not his or her head. The politics grows out of the story, not the other way around. And the politics is enmeshed in such human form that it betrays all the mixed motives that we possess. Malouf's latest book of short stories, *Every Move You Make* (2006), has this quality, especially his rendition of two boys going bush together in 'The Valley of Lagoons', but I am more concerned with how he deals with racism.

There is another lesser known Australian of Lebanese background who is also writing in this organic form. Jad el Hage's recent novel, *The Myrtle Tree* (Banipal 2007), is a gentle exploration of life in a Lebanese village. While it addresses all the traditional problems we associate with Lebanon – factionalism, violence, tribalism, religious wars and so on – it does so from the home of an elder, barely mentioning religion. It is a superb example of talking politics without talking about it.

The Myrtle Tree reminds me of two other Arab books that achieve the same quality. One is the novel by the Sudanese writer Tayeb Salih, *Season of Migration to the North* (1969, Penguin 2003), in which, long before Edward Said, Salih expresses how an 'oriental' experiences London. Or maybe, more correctly, how London experiences 'an oriental'. The other is the superb memoir by Palestinian poet Mourid Barghouti, *I Saw Ramallah* (1997, translated into English, published by Random House 2003), which tells of Barghouti's return to his home town in occupied Palestine after he left in 1966 to go to university in Cairo and was denied re-entry for thirty years. *I Saw Ramallah* expresses more than any other book I have read what it means to be an exile from your own land. Such is the power of writing in truth. The hand that wrote *I Saw Ramallah* reached straight out from the page and grabbed my throat and gripped me for the entire reading of the book.

In *Us and Them*, my own recent tentative step into writing, I have tried to stay true to a felt need, not to a propaganda imperative. Starting as a journalist at the *Sydney Morning Herald*, writing was my first love. When Random House suggested a book of memoirs, I liked the idea. But something didn't quite fit with my conception of myself. Returning from the Middle East, I knew I had to write about my own journey of understanding of the past five or more years about 'the other' in the shape of the demonised Arab, Muslim and Palestinian people. I felt vulnerable and exposed – not a journalist's normal stance. But it was one I had to take to express what I had seen and been through. For once, I was a journalist/writer refusing to hide behind the shield of anonymity. I hope to continue this exploration.

Conclusion

Writers have been drawn to issues of justice from the beginning of writing. What is fair, what is right, what is just? Lives have depended on the answers. In South America, writers died by the thousands in the 1960s through to the 1980s defending their freedom and defending the lives of other writers and political prisoners. Rudolfo Walsh was a well-known investigative journalist in Buenos Aires. In March 1977 he sent an 'Open Letter' to the Argentinian military junta on behalf of the thousands of writers 'disappearing' and being tortured for their words in military concentration camps across the nation. Walsh disappeared the next day and was never seen again. His story of bravery in the defence of writers has been repeated over and over again.

What shall we write? In these times of fear and loathing, especially of 'the other', what shall we write? There is no single answer to that question. Ken Loach answers it with his films. Bertolt Brecht answered it with plays. Mahmoud Darwish, the Palestinian national poet, answers it in verse. The Russian journalist Anna Politkovskaya answered it with her investigations and is now dead. We in Australia will speak when the moment arrives for each of us, but let that speaking not be forced, head-driven or simply propaganda. Writers are not disconnected from the times, but nor are we prisoners of them.

In praise of political fiction

Rosie Scott

I'm particularly interested in fiction that is concerned with social justice. For the sake of brevity, I'll use the term 'political fiction' to describe this genre. One definition of political fiction is that it works as a mouthpiece for the dispossessed in a society, speaks to them and for them, and is, as a result, one important source for the predominant myths and moral tone of a community.

Everyone has at least one personal example of the volcanic influence of non-fiction books, from Germaine Greer's *The Female Eunuch* to Rachel Carson's *Silent Spring*, Arundhati Roy's *The Algebra of Infinite Justice* and the recent crop of books about the Iraq war and the Bush government, or can point to important changes in our historical perspective because of the work of Australian historians like Manning Clark, Henry Reynolds and Tony Kevin and journalists such as David Marr and Marian Wilkinson. But it is difficult to prove that Rosario Murillo's poetry spurred on the Sandinistas, or that in Australia Eliot Perlman's *Three Dollars* raised consciousness of homelessness, Robert Drewe's *Grace* changed people's view of mandatory detention or Judith Wright's poetry heightened awareness of conservation or the fate of Indigenous people in Australia. Fiction has a much more complicated interaction with the national psyche, but if you accept that fiction is a reflection of society, however distorted it becomes, then it seems absurd to dismiss its subtle connections with the people and social structure it springs from.

In the flowering of tired old complacencies, commonplace, second-rate and callous ideology, and the general dumbing down of Australian society, the vitality of fiction is even more necessary as an antidote to the takeover of intellectual life which has permeated Australia. It is fashionable for ideological reasons in Howard's Australia to deride the importance of writers and intellectuals and their input into the direction and tone of a society. What, after all, do such 'elites' know about making profits, or for that matter real life? This derision, of course, is made easier if fiction remains safe, assimilable, and remote from what is happening.

As Andrew McGahan said in a recent interview in the *Bulletin*: 'This no longer seems the time to be polite or indirect in fiction, or artfully diffident. It's time to confront the danger and what's going on here head on' (24 October 2006). The importance of fiction in informing public consciousness was clearly demonstrated in a survey on fiction reading in Australia published in the *Sydney Morning Herald* in September 1990. The authors noted that it was clear from letter after letter that books give some of the most satisfying and deepest experiences in people's lives. Literature emerged, and I quote from one letter, 'as a cultural anchor in a world made stormy by the soulless'. The intellectual, moral, political and aesthetic climate can either foster or discourage the creation of this kind of fiction in many subtle ways.

In Australia it is easy to see how the political, cultural and ideological bias encouraged by the Howard government affects the writing of political fiction. Our political and cultural landscape is dominated by what is now arguably the most influential political fiction of all – carefully crafted spin – that poisonous language which muffles the truth and plays so effectively on our fears, aspirations and prejudices. It is no surprise that the Howard government has spent more money on spin than any other government in Australian history, and very successfully.

Our harsh sedition laws were put in place by Philip Ruddock, with only a few modifications as a sop to the storm of protest from the legal community and from writers. Under these sedition provisions a person could theoretically be jailed for seven years for saying that the military invasion of Iraq was wrong, or for supporting the Iraqi people. As Neville Wran, ex-premier of New South Wales, pointed out, the legislation 'potentially turns legitimate political activity and dissent into *prima facie* criminality'.[1] It is no longer a defence to say that stating a fact is not the same as intending to urge someone to violence. In such a political climate writers and journalists, as well as artists, musicians, actors, satirists, filmmakers and cartoonists, become afraid to be outspoken and start self-censoring.

The recent enhancement of ASIO's powers as outlined in the Anti-Terrorism Bill of 2005 means, in effect, that journalists who in the course of their work are thought to have some information about a person in which ASIO has an interest may be arrested and interrogated, forced to break their confidentiality or even jailed if deemed to be uncooperative or fail to answer questions.

In Australia in 2006, market-driven publishers, the subtle and not so subtle political censorship, the government appointment of right-wing ideologues to important cultural institutions like the ABC and the Australia Council, the Howard government's encouragement of hysterical jingoism and dislike and fear of the elite (meaning writers and intellectuals) all combine to create a fearful and conservative literary climate. It is paradoxical, however, that this extreme constraint may also in the end encourage the emergence of a genuine, more deeply felt literature of dissent as more writers feel moved to speak out. The political fiction of Richard Flanagan and Andrew McGahan published in 2006 are just two examples.

In the publishing world, the market reigns supreme; books are published on the final say-so of the marketing departments and on the previous financial record of the author. In the world of the bottom line, only books that will definitely make a profit are considered for publication. Publishing is now even more than ever about winners and losers, markets and money, so that the quality of writing and ideas has slipped down in the scale of importance.

The value put on the 'winners' in society has always been a very ambiguous one and is summarised well by a comment of Kurt Vonnegut's. He said that the 'single religion of winners is a harsh interpretation of Darwinism, which argues that it is the will of the universe that only the fittest should survive. One should behave heartlessly towards losers if one hopes to survive. All the rest is hokum.'[2] Judging by what has happened in Australia, this is a pretty fair summary of the prevailing political ethos.

The influence of a fiction writer like Vonnegut on my own thinking is of course no accident and illustrates these ideas nicely: that there is, first of all, such a thing as political fiction that can change people's minds; and that, when political events outdistance the literary imagination, the lack of that imagination leaves a vacuum at the heart of a national literature.

Tony Fomison, one of New Zealand's best-known painters, said in a remarkable interview just before he died: 'To have a life means that you have an obligation to look after all species, which include other people. I have had a vision of a shared society which informs and inspires all my art.'[3] Political fiction has a similar basis, and I want to suggest that as a body of work it can create important life-sustaining myths that provide a healthy counter-balance to the superficial, the destructive and the heartless, which are always present in society and now, perhaps more than at any other period, in Australian history. This is not prescriptive, because writers cannot simply set out to write good political fiction as a logical exercise or because they are disturbed about a particular issue. As Oscar Wilde said: 'A work of art comes from the fact that the author is what he is. It has nothing to do with the fact that people want what they want.'

In my view, writing that is genuinely political has to be accessible, truthful, dangerous to the unjust order it reflects, and always relevant and inspirational to the lives of ordinary people, as well as sophisticated readers. For these reasons, political fiction is not easy to write and remains a minority genre in the literature of most countries. It seems to me that unless a few writers are achieving it, and providing a healthy antidote to the bias in society, the national literature as a whole is subtly affected.

Political fiction is not tractor art, propaganda or left- or right-wing novels with sympathetic characters and lots of political conversations, because of course fiction can be about politics without being political fiction. It's more complicated than that.

I'm talking about a particular sensibility that drenches the whole work and flows from a coherent vision. When I think of 'political' writers I admire – a range as diverse as Charles Dickens, Garcia Lorca, Pablo Neruda, Simone de Beauvoir, Marilyn French, Whitman, Judith Wright, Margaret Walker, Grace Paley, Gabriel Garcia Marques, Alice Walker, Zora Thurston Hughes, Nadine Gordimer, Lionel Fogarty, Tom Keneally, Dorothy Hewett, Patricia Grace – I think the one quality they all have in common is passion. There is also most likely a love and respect for the so-called 'losers' of society, anger at injustice, and a humorous acceptance of human frailty. There is a luminescence in their writing which is almost overwrought sometimes, but which informs every line and produces brilliant language. For me personally, reading that sort of writing feeds a hunger I have for literary extremes, unashamed commitment, courage, and an instantly recognisable relevance.

One of the best examples of a literary community where writing is literally the voice of the people is of course in South America. Pablo Neruda's poetry, for instance, is irradiated with love, suffering, optimism, a wry humour and intelligence, all expressed in stunningly evocative language. For me, his poem 'I'm explaining a few things' is the literary equivalent of Picasso's *Guernica*. Neruda consciously attempted to speak to the ordinary people of his country and believed that his ability to do so was a privilege.

In the introduction to the Penguin edition of Neruda's selected poems, Jean Franco compares Neruda to the Orphic poets Dante, Milton, Whitman and Hugo, because his work is also bound by a coherent vision of people and their society. Franco writes: 'Just as we cannot separate Dante and Milton from their theology, or Hugo and Whitman from the idea of progress and democracy, so we cannot take Neruda's poetry without his vision of unalienated people or justice and equality on earth.' Or as Neruda himself writes:

> And you will ask: why doesn't his poetry
> speak of dreams and leaves
> and the great volcanoes of his native land?
> Come and see the blood in the streets
> come and see
> the blood in the streets
> Come and see the blood
> in the streets!

At one extreme, political fiction can be literally dangerous for the writers and readers. Introducing an anthology of Central American poets, entitled *Volcan*,[4] the editor notes that many of the poets included had since been tortured or killed, and that their poems had only survived by being passed from hand to hand. He describes the long tradition they were carrying on from past poet-warriors, men and women who had fought the early struggles against European and North American invasions of their country and, in the case of women, the patriarchal oppressions of their society. In a closing statement, which has all the force of simple truth, the editor describes the anthology as a contact bomb, ready to explode.

In Eastern Europe, where poets and playwrights are now heroes or in government after years of danger and despair, from Russia to Iran to China, where authoritarianism, injustice and poverty go hand in hand, it is often the fiction writers who are seen as dangerous by the authorities, surely the ultimate proof of the political potency of their work. A quick glance at Nobel prize laureates shows (apart from the fact that 80 per cent of them are men) how many of them were writing political fiction. Many writers have become political outcasts, been imprisoned or been executed simply because they were or are writing dissenting views, as the copious files of PEN International attest. Now that the American social realist writers like Dos Passos, Steinbeck and Lewis are dusty, unread classics, it is easy to forget the shock impact they had on American society at the time. It is not until relatively recently that the simple fact of a woman taking up a pen to write fiction was seen as a provocative political act.

The kind of intensity of that sort of life, lived in the shadow of violent death and extreme poverty, and even the credo that fiction can be a political act has as yet little relation to writers' lives in Australia and New Zealand, though Maori, Aboriginal and feminist writers are much closer to that kind of political commitment. We can be grateful that our poetry is not passed from hand to hand like a grenade but sits forever in our bookshops and that our novels are prescribed reading in schools. White Australian writers still have some security. Many of us are middle class and reasonably well provided for, and of course the same can be said for some of the political writers I have mentioned. Being hunted is not necessarily a prerequisite for good political fiction – that is as absurd as the starving-in-the-attic myth. But by the same token, being on the winning side all the time can make things go a little blurry. It is partly this institutionalised comfort, this lack of passion here which means that a lot of our fiction is simply not reflecting all the aspirations and hungers of our society. Visiting Czech writer Josef Skvorecky said once in Sydney that it is difficult for a person who lives in a country where there are no wars, no censorship and no secret police to become a great writer.

However, once the Howard government began to imprison asylum-seekers in detention camps for long periods, concern about censorship, arbitrary laws and the abuse of human rights began to surface once again in our 'lucky country'.

Another Country, an anthology of the work of detained writers, came out of the work of Sydney PEN and a newly formed committee on Writers in Detention, which was made up of myself, Annette Hughes and Tom Keneally. Since 1921, International PEN has campaigned for writers imprisoned, tortured and harassed in countries everywhere in the world. In 2001, we in Australian PEN realised that we had to look to our own backyard in Howard's Australia. We had discovered that there were writers who had been imprisoned for years in our midst. They were living in terribly harsh conditions, without charge and without trial. They were always in fear of being deported to the countries they had fled, where in many cases a worse fate awaited them. We had a few aims: to give these writers a voice and to affirm their gift by publishing their work; to allow Australians to read first-hand the facts of the camps by the persuasive means of literature; to have a written record of the excesses of this shameful policy; and to try to effect the release of these detainees. So the idea of an anthology was born.

We called it *Another Country* because the privatised detention camps were operated like fiefdoms, with their own laws and values, both of which were often quite alien to mainstream Australia. We hoped the anthology would give the Australian public an alternative to the biased media coverage which has consistently and wrongly suggested that all asylum-seekers are terrorists who throw their children into the sea, have narrow-minded and fanatical religious beliefs and are 'queue-jumpers'.

We set about the long and complicated task of trying to contact the writers. It took over a year to find the networks, get in touch with writers in the detention camps, collect their work, and have it translated and ready for publication. In doing so, we could not have succeeded without the network of women who devote hundreds of hours to refugee issues and to the personal fate of the detainees themselves. In many cases, it was their support and affirmation that kept the writers from despair. The camps are dedicated to destroying the detainees' spirits – and these women set about restoring them.

Mohsen Zand, an Iranian poet, contributor to *Another Country* and ex-detainee, wrote of these people:

> You are the only hope after God
> and you are the light in the darkness of Australian 'democracy'.
> You are the ones who are left.
> We hear the voice of conscience through your mouth.

One Iraqi poet, an opponent of Saddam Hussein, who lost two sons as a result of Saddam's political activities, and was imprisoned in Australian camps for five years, said to me: 'We have been put through hell here in Australia, but we have also met with the kindest people on earth.'

We were warned by an ex-detainee, Human Rights award-winner Dr Aamer Sultan, that detainees had been so traumatised and damaged by the camps that rejection of their work could be the final straw. We realised this was going to be no simple literary anthology. For many, these words and stories were a matter of life and death. Aamer's words proved to be prophetic.

The quality of writing we received was beyond our wildest hopes. It was like receiving vivid and compelling messages from some unnamed country on our borders where despair, depression and suicide were the norm. Some writers found that publication of their work gave them new hope and affirmation, some were moved to write for the first time to express their suffering and to reach out to Australians and tell them what was happening.

David Malouf wrote of *Another Country*: 'Listening to these voices is like looking into the mirror. They come not from strangers but from men and women who are already fellow citizens, close and clearly recognisable, of the same world we live in.'

During the time that this work was collected we also began to correspond with the writers, and wrote supporting letters on behalf of Sydney PEN and in some cases of PEN International to advocate for their release. We enabled many of them to join Sydney PEN while they were still in detention. Other branches of Australian PEN were also deeply involved in their own cases.

The first edition of the book was launched by Claudia Karvan at Gleebooks, and it sold out that night. This edition was completed with the help of Lyneve Rappell and Matthew Richardson of Halstead Press. Tom Keneally and I had been guest editors of this *Southerly* edition of *Another Country* under the editorship of David Brooks. There was a second *Southerly* edition of the anthology which sold out that year, followed by a third, expanded edition by Halstead Press which came out in 2005.

Another Country has been very successful, garnering much publicity for the issue of asylum-seekers with numerous events all over Australia. These events, panels and demonstrations involved speakers such as Ariel

Dorfman, David Malouf, Bryan Brown, Rachel Ward and Claudia Karvan, and were covered by both national and international media. The launch of the third edition of *Another Country* was an event unique in Australian literary history, being held outside Baxter Detention Centre. Surrounded on all sides by desert, with the forbidding edifice of Baxter as the backdrop, it was attended by 100 people from all over Australia and was addressed by Christine Rau. Sarath Amarasinghe smuggled out a message: 'My dear friends, I am very happy to hear about your book launch in front of Baxter. My heartfull regards to all of you.'

An ABC arts program was made about *Another Country*, and there were positive editorials, articles and reviews both in Australia and overseas. The UNHCR (the United Nations Refugee Agency), International PEN and the International Coalition on the Detention of Refugees, Migrants and Asylum Seekers, bought copies for distribution and research. Because an increasing number of western governments are adopting the punitive Howard model of detaining asylum-seekers, the idea of the Sydney Writers in Detention committee has been studied with great interest by International PEN. Branches in Germany have started their own similar committees.

In 2004 Australian PEN received the Community Human Rights Award. The judges credited PEN with raising awareness of asylum-seeker issues within the Australian conscience, and, singling out the Writers in Detention committee and *Another Country*, said it was able to bring national and international pressure to bear in seeking the release of asylum-seekers in detention. And best of all, we were able to help to secure the release of all of the contributors by supporting them in PEN's name by letter-writing, lobbying, organising public demonstrations and fundraising.

One such writer was Tony Zandavar, a particularly gifted Iranian poet whose poems I read at many gatherings throughout Australia. I first heard of Tony when Annise Gaffney, a refugee advocate, wrote to me in May 2003: 'Enclosed is a poem by a gentle intelligent Iranian man now into his fifth year of detention. He is no longer capable of this or any other type of writing as he is now paralysed by his depression and struggles to communicate in any way.' Later she wrote again:

> He is a wonderful guy and it breaks my heart to have been witness to his deterioration over the past couple of years as his hope for any kind of future has been stripped away. He lives with the constant terror of deportation and forced return to the danger from which he escaped. There is no doubt in my mind that if he could safely return home he would have done so long ago. As well as watching his friends slowly unravelling around him, for almost 5 years now he has lived in these dreadful circumstances witnessing suicide attempts – slashed wrists, hanging and the ongoing acts of self-harm by people driven to the brink by despair and hopelessness.
>
> When I told him his poem had been selected but that a little bit of rephrasing would be necessary, he told me he would try to write a couple of others. As I have explained, his deterioration makes it almost impossible for him to concentrate and his writing is now very confused and fragmentary but I am honouring his wishes and sending them to you anyway because I know what a mammoth undertaking it was for him to write them.
>
> Your interest in his work has resurrected a little spark of interest and provided a small purpose in otherwise empty days. I know Tony has continued to write a little more and I know that is entirely due to your encouragement.

The Writers in Detention committee of Sydney PEN became involved in Tony's case, raising money for a lawyer through donations from friends and a benefit concert. Tom and I believe he has rare gifts as a poet and that his poetry helped him to survive. There was a crowd of dedicated advocates working on his case before Sydney PEN came on the scene, but it was not until September 2004 that he was finally released. We attended his wedding some time later, which he described as the happiest day of his life, and he is now living with his Australian wife and son in Tasmania and has recently been granted a permanent visa.

A young man from Afghanistan whose experiences with war and suffering began from the age of six with the Russian invasion of his village, followed by the Taliban, who injured his mother and brothers, wrote: 'My parents decided to send me to safety by boat to Australia. Which was my second death. The Australian government put me in a hellhole and locked me up for three years.' Just after I received his story, he was admitted to Glenside, the psychiatric unit, after trying to kill himself.

Many of the writers I met in the camps had fled to Australia because their progressive views were not tolerated in their own countries. In their conversations and correspondence with me, and in their writing, they make this point over and over again in complete bewilderment. They cannot understand the treatment they have received. They had believed they were fleeing from totalitarian governments and repressive views to a liberal haven where political and religious differences were not only tolerated but celebrated. Many of them became deeply traumatised by the racist vitriol directed at them in the media and by many of the guards in the camps.

The mental illness that is endemic in the camps (a recent survey showed that clinical depression is inevitable in the camps after a certain period of time) was brought about not only by the brutal and dehumanising treatment they received but also by the senselessness of their imprisonment. What had they done wrong? Why were they being punished? Who were their judges?

Here is Cheikh Kone's account of arriving in the country he believed would help him. Cheikh is a Muslim journalist from the Ivory Coast. After being threatened by deportation by the Australian authorities, PEN International put him in the category of 'writers at risk', a shameful first for Australia, as this is a category usually applied to writers in places like Burma, China, Turkey or Iran. Cheikh wrote:

> Two very hostile individuals confronted me without introduction. With my poor English I was able to comprehend only some of what they were saying. Who had told me to come to Australia? Didn't I know that coming here was harshly punished? I told them I was a journalist who was forced to leave the Ivory Coast because my writings had annoyed the government.

> Sometimes, I wondered what have we done to deserve such an inhumane punishment. I have seen inmates slicing themselves, sewing their lips or flying into a sharp razor wire, not because they were insane but because of the den of frustration they found themselves in. We were treated like children, our lives controlled as to when we slept or ate. For most the time, when ill we were given two panadols and ten glasses of water, regardless of the condition.
>
> Between adolescence and adulthood a political ideal called democracy caught my attention. I quickly became an advocate of this ideal believing in its great strengths. Today after almost three years' detention in a democratic country, I don't know what to believe any more.

Or as Mina, a fourteen-year-old Iraqi girl wrote in her diary, after describing a particularly traumatic demonstration in the camp which she witnessed: 'Oh God! Help us, help everyone!'

Aamer Sultan, an Iraqi doctor and political refugee, was detained for three years. He was given a Human Rights Award while still in Villawood for his work on depression there. He wrote:

> What difference would it make to them anyway [the Australian government] if the whole world chanted for us to be released, these kids growing traumatised with serious personality disorders and retarded emotional development? My reaction, my attempts to make a difference have shifted from anger, shouting, advocating, networking and humble individual support to that of feeling simply disempowered and helplessly shamed and depressed. Totally disillusioned about the western world humanitarian utopia I used to believe in.

Sarath Amarasinghe, another contributor, courageously published an outspoken newsletter called *Baxter News* for some years while he was still in detention – in his words, 'to expose the inhumanity of the camps'. In PEN's annual 'Day of the Imprisoned Writer' a writer in detention is commemorated by an Empty Chair, and Sarath Amarasinghe, like Cheikh Kone, Dr Sultan and Tony Zandavar, was honoured in this way by Sydney PEN.

For all of us involved in compiling *Another Country* it was a roller-coaster ride, with all the worries, sorrows and responsibility of knowing that we were working for people unjustly imprisoned, desperate and depressed after years of incarceration, and also knowing that they could be deported back to the dangers from which they fled. For me it was like travelling without a map, in Kafkaesque territory, where there were no landmarks or road signs, and a continual feeling of threat on the horizon. Department of Immigration and Multicultural and Indigenous Affairs (DIMIA) law or lack of it is classic totalitarian stuff – labyrinthine, agonisingly slow and often cruel and senseless, and, because of this arbitrariness and lack of guidelines, extremely difficult to follow or abide by logically. The dangers of this *modus operandi* have become increasingly clear since it has been revealed that a number of people have been detained unlawfully, including Australian citizens.

Readers of *Another Country* were moved to action, many public events grew up around it, national and international organisations used it for reference and it was bought by university, school and public libraries. As a form of political fiction, it directly affected the lives and thinking of the writers themselves as well as the readers. As the *Sydney Morning Herald* editorial noted: 'Books like *Another Country* provide an alternative view – that asylum-seekers are people rather than numbers, that Australia provides punishment rather then refuge and children detained suffer enormously' (18 May 2004).

The period in Australian history when the Howard government enforced the imprisonment of thousands of innocent people in brutal camps will go down as one of our darkest. But, like all periods of suffering, there are extraordinary stories of heroism, love, humour and courage as well as stories of cruelty, grief, despair and barbarism. Many of these stories are as yet known only to the refugee advocates and the detainees themselves.

Our experiences with *Another Country* proved again the power of art and literature to move people, to allow us to see into one another's hearts, to foster compassion and understanding, to inspire political action, and to work in a way that almost nothing else does.

Australian writers have had a long history of social concern and commitment, from the storytelling traditions of the first inhabitants, to people like Lawson, Prichard, Wright, Oodgeroo, Keneally, Hewett and Grenville. Their work celebrates and criticises the society in which they live, and their knowledge and love of Australia, their ability and desire to speak to their own, was and is an important aspect of the growth of a healthy national literature and political fiction. But it is now, when American cultural and political influences show no signs of diminishing in Australia and the complacencies and desolation of a dominant right-wing political philosophy continue to flourish under the Howard government, that the kind of strong, relevant and dangerous fiction I have been talking about is most needed.

Jose Urtecho, a poet from Nicaragua, the country where poetry workshops were set up in every town just weeks after the Sandinistan victory, has suggested that in advanced capitalist countries poetry (political by its very nature, in his eyes) is 'constrained, possessed by the rigours of actuality, merchandised in a world which is not made for poets, but against poets'.

James Baxter said that it was a 'sense of grief' that helped him to write poems and that 'in a sense his poems sprang out of a quarrel with the status quo'. He added: 'A writer cannot avoid the task of exploring and understanding the threefold aspect of the modern world – monotony, atrocity, anarchy – if he has not first done this.'

I have always thought that the lightning rod of a national literature is located somewhere amongst the outsiders of a society, the minorities, the dispossessed and the oppressed. It was Graham Greene who said that 'genuine culture is always in opposition'. I think that these are the people who often have a greater if more painful insight into the real workings of their society.

As Rebecca Solnit says of political writing in her wonderful book *Hope in the Dark: The Untold History of People Power*:

> An essay, a book, is one statement in a long conversation that you could call culture or history; you are answering something or

> questioning something that may have fallen silent long ago, and the response to your words may come long after you'd gone and never reach your ears.[5]

Frantz Fanon, in his classic *The Wretched of the Earth*, expresses the idea in his usual inimitable style:

> We must join them in that fluctuating movement which they [the oppressed] are just giving shape to, and which, as soon as it has started, will be the signal for everything to be called in question. Let there be no mistake about it: it is to this zone of occult instability where the people dwell that we must come: and it is there that our souls are crystallised and that our perceptions and our lives are transfused with light.[6]

In my own view, I think of the best political fiction as work where love is considered important, the world a place to be celebrated and passionately fought for, where there is humour, optimism and sensuality as well as a fierce, compassionate gaze at the ugliness, grotesqueness and injustice of life.

Political fiction is not a mechanistic reactive process, but a remarkably complex and imaginative feat of writing which reflects society accurately and compassionately, disturbs, sustains and is usually motivated by a love for fellow beings and anger at injustice. It was Kurt Vonnegut who suggested that the motto for winners should be 'ignore agony' and perhaps in a nutshell that is the function and the greatest achievement of the best political fiction – to bring agony to our attention with rage, wit, style, compassion and love.

Just poetry

Noel Rowe

> He who takes his stand in relation shares in a reality, that is, in a being that neither merely belongs to him nor merely lies outside him. All reality is an activity in which I share without being able to appropriate for myself. Where there is no sharing there is no reality. The more direct the contact with the Thou, the fuller is the sharing.
>
> Martin Buber [1]

When *Bringing Them Home* was being discussed in Federal Parliament and politicians were deciding whether or not the nation could or should make an apology, I kept thinking about a poem. I even gave way to fantasy, imagining what would happen if that poem were taken into the House and read. Would it help anyone feel and understand that justice involves more than abstract notions of equity and debt, and much, much more than the economics of reparation? Would it help anyone appreciate that, whatever their strict legal status, emotions, bodies and stories contribute to our moral imaginations and are all part of the poetics of justice?

The poem I had in mind was Eva Johnson's 'A Letter to My Mother', which begins:

I not see you long time now, I not see you long time now
White fulla bin take me from you, I don't know why
Give me to Missionary to be God's child.
Give me new language, give me new name
All time I cry, they say – 'that shame'
I go to city down south, real cold
I forget all them stories, my Mother you told
Gone is my spirit, my dreaming, my name
Gone to these people, our country to claim
They gave me white mother, she give me new name
All time I cry, she say – 'that shame'
I not see you long time now, I not see you long time now.[2]

Lamenting how for its speaker 'A culture [. . .] was replaced by a mission', the poem holds to a belief that 'One day your dancing, your dreaming, your song / Will take me your Spirit back where I belong'. It demands that the 'aliens who rule' will protect what they do not understand; it longs for that moment 'When I hear you my Mother give me my Name'. So it expresses a difficult ambiguity: at one level it tells a stolen generations story; at another level it says that such a story remains untold until mother and daughter find each other.

How does this poem incorporate a poetic of justice? To answer this question in such a way as to give credit to both poetry and justice, it is necessary to do more than ascertain whether or not it is a factual account of a child taken, legally if immorally, from her mother, to do more than assess, as if this can be done empirically, what amount of emotional damage has been done. It is necessary to enter the separation that is embodied in the poem's address, as we feel the space opening between the speaker's feelings, so definite and so intensely present, and her uncertainty about where her mother is. This is keyed in the opening line, which acts as a refrain throughout the poem. 'I not see you long time now' is, in its effect, more complex than first impressions might suggest. The I–you address provides a fundamental understanding of the relational self, and with that a relational understanding of justice. This is picked up when the speaker acknowledges that she remains incomplete until she hears her mother name her. The 'not see you' establishes the absence of the relational and reciprocal, but it also echoes the institutional imperative, the way in which policy said to mother and daughter 'you will not see each other'. Without necessarily conceptualising what the poem is doing, many listeners will hear how it turns 'long time' into the time of longing and respond with something like moral sympathy. In these ways, standing somewhere between elegy and protest, using a separated address that embodies the spiritual, emotional and physical experience of dislocation, the poem asks for justice. Anyone who responds to what the poem is doing (and it is doing more than what it is saying) is unlikely to start adding up how much 'sorry' might cost the government in compensation, unlikely to dispute whether stories and their feelings constitute admissible evidence. Anyone who responds is more likely to see that justice needs to be capable of doing much more than pronounce 'that shame'. Justice is not as simple as some isolable arithmetical calculation of what is due to and what is adequate for an individual who has wronged or been wronged. Justice needs to be responsible for the ways in which it is itself involved in activities analogous to giving and naming. Justice is as much an act of reciprocated respect as of retribution, and respect ought not be calculated. But the poem was never read in the House on the hill.

One Australian poet who did more than most to nurture respect for Indigenous history was Judith Wright. Her commitment to Indigenous rights is well known, as is her expression of this in poems such as 'Bora Ring', 'At Cooloolah', 'Nigger's Leap, New England', 'Two Dreamtimes' and 'For a Pastoral Family'.[3] These poems make it clear that she was troubled by the ambiguities of her own family's history, in particular the way in which pastoral settlement depended on dispossession. In 'Bora Ring', 'Nigger's Leap, New England' and 'At Cooloolah' she addresses repressed memories of Aboriginal deaths, employing an image of something shameful buried under the white narration of land, waiting to shipwreck history and its claims. In 'Bora Ring' she also uses line-endings to ensure that the repressed resurfaces; as she names those aspects of Indigenous culture that have been lost, she positions them just before the end-of-line pause, so that for a moment they are strongly present in the reader's breath and mind. This is evident in the poem's opening stanza:

> The song is gone; the dance
> is secret with the dancers in the earth,
> the ritual useless, and the tribal story
> lost in an alien tale. (CP 8)

Whatever the state of Indigenous ritual, the poem's ritual is not as useless as it pretends. Wright subtly turns absence into presence and enacts the haunted memory she is talking about. This technique is then used at the end of the poem to express 'an unsaid word'. Telling of how a white settler rides over his subdued landscape, the poem records a ghostly and accusatory apparition:

> Only the rider's heart
> halts at a sightless shadow, an unsaid word
> that fastens in the blood the ancient curse,
> the fear as old as Cain. (CP 8)

In 'At Cooloolah', naming herself 'a stranger, come of a conquering people', the speaker confesses she is 'made uneasy, for an old murder's sake' (CP 140). She also unsettles assumptions about ownership of land:

> Those dark-skinned people who once named Cooloolah
> knew that no land is lost or won by wars,
> for earth is spirit: the invader's feet will tangle
> in nets there and his blood be thinned by fears. (CP 140)

Ambitious, fast designs on land and history are undercut from the beginning: the poem opens with the image of a blue crane that has fished at Cooloolah 'longer than our centuries' and is 'the certain heir' of the place.

Wright's relational understanding of justice is then made explicit in the way the poem ends: even as she establishes a fundamental choice between justified possession and the 'arrogant guilt' and 'fear' that underpin illegitimate possession, she connects justice and love:

> White shores of sand, plumed reed and paperbark,
> clear heavenly levels frequented by crane and swan –
> I know that we are justified only by love,
> but oppressed by arrogant guilt, have room for none.
>
> And walking on clean sand among the prints
> of bird and animal, I am challenged by a driftwood spear
> thrust from the water; and, like my grandfather,
> must quiet a heart accused by its own fear. (CP 141)

This ending initiates a critique of *terra nullius*: her prints are not the first, the sand is not 'clean' in the way a blank page might be; rather than assume ownership she has to learn to walk with bird and animal, in particular with the blue crane who does not so much own as belong in the place. Wright believed Australians would only belong in and to the land when they learned to love it. In 'For a Pastoral Family' (CP 406 ff.), dealing more directly with her own family's claims to ownership of land, Wright evokes a melancholy irony in describing how her forerunners:

> [. . .] took over as if by right a century and a half
> in an ancient difficult bush. And after all
> the previous owners put up little fight,
> did not believe in ownership, and so were scarcely human. (CP 406)

She goes on to confess how her generation did not know or did not want to know the 'really deplorable deeds' that 'happened out of our sight, allowing us innocence.' She then exposes the way in which law was used to protect this fiction of innocence, allowing the conquerors to 'enter a plea: Not

Guilty'. A decade later, this plea was often entered by those who argued against the Howard government saying sorry to the stolen generations (as if one were not responsible unless one were to blame).

All this is familiar to most readers of Wright's poetry. But these poetic statements about injustices are not what constitute her poetic of justice and reconciliation. Her poetic of justice is grounded in images, tones, speaking positions that create a relational ethic. In 'Two Dreamtimes' she occupies an uncertain position: she is troubled by a childhood in which she seemed innocent of, ignorant of, the racism going on around her; she revisits an ambiguity fundamental to her life (and) writing, that between possession and dispossession, by confessing that 'they hadn't told me the land I loved / was taken out of your hands' (CP 315); she acknowledges the loss of country, culture and dreaming, comparing this to (though not equating it with) the loss of country caused by anti-environmental practices and policies. The poem, however, does more than state its case; it enacts a relationship. All that is said is said as a conversation, a sister-to-sister talk, incorporating stories Kath Walker[4] has told her and giving back Wright's troubled stories of settlement. And it opens with thanks for story:

> Kathy my sister with the torn heart,
> I don't know how to thank you
> for your dreamtime stories of joy and grief
> written on paperbark. (CP 315)

The entire poem sustains this I–you attitude. This in turn is reinforced by an image, in the fourth stanza, of the two women talking at a kitchen table. The address that is the poem depends on memories of stories that Walker told Wright. These stories have nurtured understanding between the two women, even though understanding cannot exist for Wright without guilt and grief:

> you brought me to you some of the way
> and came the rest to meet me,

> over the desert of red sand
> came from your lost country
> to where I stand with all my fathers,
> their guilt and righteousness. (CP 316)

At one level, then, the poem reminds us that justice occurs within story and within community. Even so, those who do not agree with its propositions might happily dismiss it as the work of a greenie indulging in a self-satisfying show of guilt. Poems are always vulnerable to this kind of dismissal, much as peace and reconciliation are always vulnerable to power play. This poem is, however, too ambiguous for such an unfair dismissal. Even as it conjures the image of two women sharing at the kitchen table, it acknowledges a knife between them: 'I am born of the conquerors, / you of the persecuted.' (CP 317) That fundamental inequity cannot be undone by soft intention, nor by recognising 'If we are sisters, it's in this – our grief for a lost country' (CP 316). So the speaker turns the knife, reversing power as if somehow to reverse history. The women have, finally, to relate in the space between the knife and the poem. The sister–sister relationship has to acknowledge and perhaps negotiate the conqueror–persecuted relationship. The round-table conversation may be a model for justice, but this does not mean the knotty legacies of history are easily untied:

> My shadow-sister, I sing to you
> from my place with my righteous kin,
> to where you stand with the Koori dead,
> 'Trust none – not even poets.'
>
> The knife's between us, I turn it round,
> the handle to your side,
> the weapon made from your country's bones.
> I have no right to take it.

But both of us die as our dreamtime dies.
I don't know what to give you
for your gay stories, your sad eyes,
but that, and a poem, sister. (CP 318)

Which is, finally, more effective: the knife or the poem? Wright does not quite resolve the problem she raises. While 'sister' gets the last word, it is no guarantee of justice. Similarly, the gift of the poem is presented as an inadequate response to Walker's stories. Nevertheless, this ending does shift their relationship from the economy of rights to the economy of gift. It is as if the poem realises that, while it is absolutely necessary to recognise rights, such recognition needs also a final generosity of spirit if it is to summon the just heart. If it is to have efficacy, the recognition of human rights depends on the capacity to give what is due.

Another poem to use a table as metaphor is Rosemary Dobson's 'Cultural Meeting'.[5] The poem deals with two meetings: a meeting of some committee addressed by a writer in exile who 'speaks for those forgotten in camps and prisons' (CP 162) and a cross-cultural meeting which occurs when the speaker, entering the writer's story, recognises and sympathises with his hunger for home. This sympathy is partly evoked by Dobson's poetic, her awareness that words will never satisfy, and partly by the way that poetic plays out politically. The speaker may have a moment of cross-cultural sympathy, but it is 'Afterwards', over a meal, and it is unlikely to make any difference to a committee full of people. Dobson will elsewhere call 'bystanders' those who miss the moment. Although her writing often deals with what she calls 'fugitive annunciations',[6] Dobson's poetic is also relational. In her sequence 'The Continuance of Poetry', she celebrates poetry's capacity to move between cultures. In one of the poems from the sequence, 'Translations under the Trees', she suggests that arts such as painting and poetry can cross borders and change imaginations, can make another language:

Poems blow away like pollen,
Find distant destinations,

Can seed new songs
In another language. (CP 185)

Poetry moves between words, between languages, between peoples. It does not hold meaning; it releases it.

There is, then, an uncertainty, or unknowing, always waiting at the borders of Dobson's writing. It makes for discretion. It also makes for humility. There is no room for imperialist epistemology, because meaning is never made entirely present, never entirely subdued to the mind. There is always a sense of something like an active horizon that separates and joins what is brought into a poem and what stays beyond it. One of the strongest expressions of this is found in 'Over the Frontier', a poem about how poetry and art emerge between being and non-being and carry with them a memory of, which is also a hope for, that place on the other side of existence, that desire that keeps poetry and art always next to nothingness.

And the poem that exists
will never equal the poem that does not exist.
Trembling, it crosses the frontier at dawn
from non-being to being
carrying a small banner,
bearing a message,

bringing news of the poem that does not exist,
that pulses like a star, red and green, no-colour,
blazing white against whiteness. (CP 129)

Perhaps uncertainty is important in the quest for justice: the invitatory other, the one who asks for justice, is always beyond what can be given. This need not mean, however, that justice has always to be subjected to cynicism and doubt. Inadequate as they might be, the moral and legal practices of justice can still be sufficient to protect principles of equality and freedom. To say justice is likely to be inadequate – even if compensation and reparation could be somehow financially exact, judgments can never quite take account of feelings, bodies, time – is not to say that it cannot still be possible and authentic. Perhaps justice, like poetry, also mediates between being and non-being and has to bear knowing how it does not exist. Perhaps justice has to admit that, like poetry, it is a word held up against death.

Dobson's poetry is profoundly elegiac.[7] This is not surprising, given her interest in the relation of being to non-being. She has written some remarkable pieces in which she seems prepared to look death in the face, as if to give it respect, to get it right. These poems include 'One Section' (CP 12), 'In a Strange House' (CP 160), 'Being Called For' (CP 161) and 'The Almond-tree in the King James Version' (CP 205). In these poems she does not abstract death; she represents it as something that happens from within the body. Nor does she see death as a matter of complaint or regret; she gives it due respect as something that asks of the body that it finally pay its dues to time.

Perhaps Dobson's poetry can remind justice that it too participates in elegy. Justice, as practised, seems to be predicated on loss. Whether it is making judgments on matters such as land rights, murder, injury claims or divorce settlements, justice is dealing with loss. Whatever is achieved in the battles for land rights, it will never fully restore land, spirit, dreaming. How often have we heard the family of a murder victim say a court decision is sufficient but that it cannot give them back the one they have lost? How often have we heard someone who has been compensated for injury say the money will help but will not give them back the life they had? How can divorce settlements pretend half the value of a house will heal the wound left when half a lifetime's love appears to have been wasted? There is always a sense of justice wanting as 'wanting' takes it between desire and lack. Justice, as experience and encounter, always involves some loss of innocence, which is perhaps not surprising: in Genesis justice enters as innocence and idealism are lost, companionable being gives way to those oppositions that sustain transgression and punishment, authority and obedience, as original grace gives way to redemption. We would perhaps like to think of justice as a moral ideal that the law itself obeys; we would perhaps like to think of justice as a poetics of equity. That is not, however, how justice usually manifests itself in practice.

Dobson's 'Cultural Meeting' knows that justice does not always get the exact measure of loss. The poem creates an oblique sympathy for one writer who cannot return home. That writer may represent all writers in exile, but he is primarily an individual sharing a meal with the speaker — and it may be his individuality rather than his representativeness that troubles the speaker's sense of justice. John D. Caputo[8] remarks that the individual is a problem for ethics because the individual is ineffable, embodying that moment when proper names escape the grasp of language, when the desire to talk about someone summons the recognition that it is impossible. Metaphysics, Caputo claims, cannot speak of the individual (who is, paradoxically, too large for metaphysics because too small), and since metaphysics contains ethics, justice is (de)constructed as an impossible obligation.[9] This poem is not, however, a philosophical argument. It is an act of sympathy, and sympathy, because it is an embodied act, responds to the individual and thus to the individual's desire for justice. To find where and how justice enters the poem, a reader has to see how, in the penultimate stanza, writer and speaker are brought together through the image of a wound:

> The cry of a word from the heart and the word is 'exile',
> It falls from the pen like a bullet-shot through the paper,
> And a charred black hole gapes like a fatal wound. (CP 163)

The image of the wound in the page displaces and unites speaker and hearer in an elegy of and for justice, a hunger that can be neither satisfied nor surrendered. It also recalls an image used earlier in the poem to suggest that writing itself never quite does justice to its subject. Thinking of the writers in exile, the speaker imagines their writing in these terms:

> Over the paper their black words driven, straggling,
> Summon from under restricting ice of absence
> The reedy singing of long-ago green water. (CP 162)

If this suggests writers in exile are like people struggling through an arctic landscape, it also prepares, by way of 'black words', for the moment when the word 'exile' will as it were pass through the paper, leaving 'a charred black hole'. In that moment the poem takes a position between aesthetic concerns with death and writing and political concerns that are real – as real as bullet holes in oppressive regimes. In that moment justice becomes a refugee, looking back to loss, unsure if asylum will be given. The poem ends with an image of the exiled writer's hands moving over breadcrumbs (an image that picks up and comments on the earlier image of his 'Hands restless, shuffling a bundle of memoranda' as he wonders how to get his message past the red tape). Hunger seems more powerful here than any hope he might receive help: 'He ate as one whose hunger would never be filled.' The poem's sympathy, its instinct for justice, includes a realisation that writer and speaker are powerless.

Another implication in Dobson's relational and elegiac poetic of justice is that it might make us wonder about the fact that justice, as practised, so often involves one party wanting to gain power over another, demanding, not offering, what is due. Justice, that is, is often imagined, at least by complainants, as no more than a legal strategy for acquiring an individual good, for satisfying personal desire. Such complainants are unlikely to be persuaded by Aquinas, who located virtue in reason and will rather than desire, related justice to the common good, and implied that justice, like charity, disposes one to will the good of the other.[10] Nor are they likely to be swayed by Portia's argument that 'earthly power doth then show likest God's / When mercy seasons justice'.[11] Yet surely justice needs to operate in relation to other virtues if there is to be a balance between individual and common goods, if it is to guarantee that it does not become an instrument of powerful, selfish interests? Whether we call them charity, mercy or compassion, surely these open, generous virtues, inasmuch as they bring together truth, detachment and love, might be the proper virtues to mediate and moderate the claims justice makes? And surely there is a sense in which justice is most deeply received as and when we are powerless?

Such questions are likely to surface for many who read the poetry of Francis Webb.[12] Suffering is at the centre of Webb's writing, where we find explorers humbled, sometimes scourged, by their failure before the unknown, a leper discarded by the Church, the martyr Maria Goretti, a homosexual disowned by family and dying in a psychiatric ward, along with another rejected because his Down's Syndrome affronts 'the wise world' with what appears to be idiocy. It is easy to see how Webb uses these figures to initiate what at first appears to be a reversal of power, and so readers can all too quickly attach Webb's poetry to a sentimentalised spirituality romancing marginality. Explorers become more human when they are broken. The leper confronts the walled city (one of Webb's favourite epistemological metaphors) with his tattered clothes, body and speech. Maria, dying after being raped and stabbed, is claimed by death and the Virgin Mary 'strangely at one'. The homosexual, a latter day Suffering Servant (Isaiah 52:13–53:12), judges and loves those who condemn him, as does Harry whose straggling attempt at words makes the Word present. What can easily be overlooked is that Webb's marginalised figures never acquire the kind of power that would, normally, see them justified. They remain powerless.

Webb seems to be interested in another kind of justice. More theological than political, more vulnerable than practical, his is a justice on the edge of absence, a justice that appears as the call made on 'us' by those who cannot effect what is due to them. His explorer Eyre becomes an Emmaus figure, entering a narrative that makes broken bread a symbol of vision (Luke 24:13–35). His leper never quite achieves eloquence, keeping his tattered tongue; even though he is transformed by a meeting with Francis of Assisi, that meeting is never dramatised in 'The Canticle' (CP 69–84), a sequence ruled over by an image of the stigmata. Maria may die a martyr, but the poem leaves her between Death, which may perform 'the embrace / Of Nothing' (CP 263), and the Woman, Mary, who may answer prayers figured in the poem through the rosary, the Angelus and the Miserere (Psalm 51). The homosexual may show 'in ugliness and agony a way to God' (CP 229), but this means he has to be kept ugly and agonised; if society stigmatises the homosexual because of his sexuality, the poem stigmatises him for the sake of sanctity. Harry's sacrament of writing may let 'us' be 'transfigured' (CP 225), but the poem's final line performs a Webbean fraction rite, breaking the Word back to flesh, history and writing as Harry's letter is directed 'to the House of no known address' (CP 225). Thus Webb's negative address brings together the ambiguities of writing and the afterlife; it keeps speech uncertain. If Webb wants justice for his characters, he is not advocating normal processes. He is figuring a mode of justice that is itself powerless, a justice that steps down. He wants justice to undergo kenosis (Philippians 2:1–11).

Webb, then, is another example of a poet who creates congruence between what he says about justice and how he says it. In his case, however, congruence is not quite achieved, because his poetry so often exercises divided speech. While it asks for compassion and justice, Webb's is also a poetry that often expects, even invites, injustice because it is so committed to the victim; and it is a poetry that constantly battles its own capacity for fascism – it is a poetry at war with itself. This means it cannot ever quite escape the oppositional, so in a sense his poetry denies even as it affirms. It wants to sacralise the homosexual but it needs to stigmatise him. It wants to make Maria Goretti as innocent as death and the Virgin Mary, but its own gaze is lewd, unable to detach itself from images of penetration. It wants the leper and Harry to challenge complacency and certitude, but confesses that it contributes to their oppression. This means that justice, in Webb's poetry, remains finally more theological desire than political opportunity. It also means that one is likely to find, in the residue left after reading, a disturbing thought: whether, precisely because it is habitually oppositional, the imaging so favoured by politicians is inclined to undermine attempts at peace and justice.

The danger in oppositional imagining is not that it generates conflict of opinion. The danger is that such imagining rests on images and metaphors that invite us to live by and within oppositions such as the Bush opposition between civilised democracy and the uncivilised (and unChristian) Other. The danger is that such images and metaphors often go unexamined, as if they had no effect on how we live. So we live in a world where the value of freedom is compromised by metaphors of force and war, where justice is something we 'get' rather than give, and where words of reconciliation are spoken from a single, empowered position. As I write, the war against terror is feeding terror; the defence of religion is making a religion of defence. The metaphors, that is, are exercising their own power, and, because they are so often metaphors of battle, that power has an enormous and unrecognised capacity for reciprocated blood.

So I have been turning more and more to poets like Wright and Dobson, because their poetry incorporates a relational and reciprocal ethic. It seems to me their poems do something more than say who deserves, who asks for, who lacks justice; they also show a way in which justice might become more approachable. I might have considered other poets. I might, for instance, have examined how James McAuley's natural law poetry sustains a hierarchical imagining with reason and will obedient to the metaphysical order, and discussed how McAuley's appeals to moral law are so often unsettled by a sense of belatedness and alienation. I might have looked at examples of postmodern poetry, which would have opened up the question of whether postmodernism undermines human rights because of its questioning of the subject, though it might also have shown that its inclination to edges, gaps and unknowns is itself an ethical activity (exposing how language itself constitutes and exercises power). I might have examined some protest poems, perhaps the obvious choice for anyone interested in how poetry addresses issues of freedom and human rights, but I doubt that many of them would, in their mode of address, incorporate a relational ethic in the manner and to the degree that Wright and Dobson do. Their poetries model those acts of power and participation that determine what we usually think of as the moral and political spheres.

I wanted to look at poems that in some way act justly, because it seems to me the need for relational and reciprocated models of political and ethical activity is urgent in a world surrendering to the poetics of terror. Here I have to confess to yet another fantasy: that the architects of terror, whether 'good' or 'evil', will give up their self-justifying oppositions and listen to Macbeth:

> If it were done when 'tis done, then 'twere well
> It were done quickly. If th' assassination
> Could trammel up the consequence, and catch,
> With his surcease, success; that but this blow
> Might be the be-all and end-all here –
> But here upon this bank and shoal of time –
> We'd jump the life to come. But in these cases
> We still have judgment here, that we but teach
> Bloody instructions, which being taught return
> To plague th' inventor. This even-handed justice
> Commends th' ingredience of our poison'd chalice
> To our own lips. (Macbeth I.vii. ll.1–12)[13]

Macbeth, of course, ignores his own counsel, becoming a student of 'bloody instructions' and a victim of their unyielding return. Macbeth, then, persuades me that the rhetoric of righteousness, which is armed with words like 'security', 'democracy', 'evil' (with or without an axis), which is ready to demonise anything that might represent 'a possible threat to our way of life', is contributing to rather than resolving the poetics of terror that creates and sustains hatred. Whatever side it makes and maintains, this rhetoric causes hatred to become pseudo-religious – in the sense that it transforms political ideas into dogmas, and then into idols. Although it might be described as wilfully relational, the rhetoric of terror is not relational in the way of the poems I have been considering. The rhetoric of terror confuses justice with power, even if it tells itself it is the power that good should exercise over evil. It does not give the sense of a waiting for, a listening to, an inclination towards the other who is addressed and is about to step into the poem, to share its space.

My journey through *Stolen*

Jane Harrison

The commission by Ilbijerri Theatre Cooperative to write the play *Stolen* was the beginning of my journey back to my own culture, a journey that I anticipate will always continue. At the time of my commission, in 1992, I was quite ignorant about the Stolen Generations, despite my Aboriginal heritage. My ignorance was fairly typical of the wider community at the time – schools certainly didn't teach the black viewpoint of our shared history, and it wasn't a topic in any of the films I had seen or the books I had read. It was absent as part of 'our' history. And although my mother grew up 'dirt poor' in a house with a dirt floor, the poverty of her circumstances making her a likely target for removal, she was never taken from her family. The extenuating factor, in my belief, was that her mother was English, and I have come across few examples of Aboriginal child removal where the mother was white. So neither my family nor myself had any direct experiences of removal.

I grew up knowing little about my culture other than knowing my mother was Aboriginal, and that I was too, but what did that mean? The few stories my mother passed down to me only highlighted the racism she experienced as a child. Living in a small country town, her father an Aboriginal shearer, she recalled being hissed at, being called 'lubra' and having stones thrown at her. Once, aged eleven, she went home and asked her mother, 'Mum, am I Aboriginal?'. Her mother replied, 'Yes', to which my mother responded, 'Then I wish I was dead'. To be Aboriginal at that time was to be the lowest of the low. My mother, incidentally, now gets, 'But you don't look Aboriginal?', which is racism too, a reverse kind that assumes you wouldn't willingly want to be Aboriginal or that, alternatively, places Aboriginal people in some anachronistic 'box' whereby certain criteria about skin colour and features must be ticked. My mother and I both get asked what 'part' of us is Aboriginal. My mother sometimes answers: 'My big toe'.

I was once asked, after speaking about *Stolen* in a public forum, why I called myself 'Aboriginal' and not 'Australian'. My reaction was one of puzzlement: why would someone think the two were mutually exclusive? I found it unsettling and wondered why some Australians treat Aboriginal people as the 'other' and expect that they should be the ones to discard their culture in order to be absorbed into the mass. Once, during a Radio National interview, I was asked: 'Do you feel more Aboriginal at the end of this [the playwriting] process?'. I was gobsmacked. After the interview the feedback from the producer was that I sounded 'defensive'. I *was* on the back foot. I found it offensive that he should assume my identification as Aboriginal was something I had to learn or tack-on, rather than an intrinsic and inseparable part of who I was. Many non-Indigenous people cannot grasp the complexities of identity, but Indigenous people generally understand that Kooris come in many colours.

My identity was always something that 'called me'. I felt it as a longing to belong, but it wasn't until my early thirties that I found a way to explore my heritage more fully. I was looking through the *Age* for a job – the advertising agency I was working for had gone bust – and I found a small ad: 'Writer/researcher wanted for Aboriginal theatre project on the Lost Children. No experience necessary.' This was my chance and I took it with feelings of elation and trepidation, the latter mainly because I questioned my suitability to be the one to document this story, and worried whether I could do such an important topic justice. I wasn't the only one with doubts. There were blackfellas associated with the play who were distrustful about my involvement – 'Who does *she* think she is?' and 'Why is *she* writing about this?'. I understood their suspicion. I had to earn my place – I still have to earn my place! But for the most part, the Aboriginal community, through my association with Ilbijerri, accepted me and my motivations for taking on the project. And Ilbijerri were fantastically supportive of me during the six-year process from commission to production (funding was the hurdle, mainly).

Once I was commissioned, my sense of responsibility kept me glued to the project, despite my doubts and what would prove to be the challenges of the project. However, by the time Ilbijerri signed the contract, I was back to being employed full-time as a copywriter in an advertising agency. I was reluctant to take on the entire role of writer/researcher but still wanted to be involved. Ilbijerri solved the problem by employing Antoinette Braybrook as the researcher and she fed me a stream of books and documents, such as the *Genocide Convention Act*. More importantly, she was a conduit to the community. She had the contacts that I, growing up distant from my extended family and community, did not. And so I became privy to some of the saddest episodes in this country's history since white settlement. As a child of a nation that condemned South Africa's apartheid, I was confronted by our own version of apartheid.

During the research phase I learnt that Australia, upon settlement by British colonists, had been deemed 'terra nullius' – empty land – sowing the seeds of our nation's denial. While I had been aware that Aborigines were not granted permission to vote until after the 1967 referendum, I was unaware that, as non-citizens, they came under the 'Flora and Fauna Act'. Aboriginal people were officially subhuman.

I learnt that around 50 000 Indigenous children had been taken from their homes or even schools by welfare officers and police, acting in accordance with state-sanctioned policies. (The figure of 50 000, hotly debated by both sides of the argument, is a moot point: five or 5000 or 50 000, it should not have happened.) The majority of children were institutionalised, although some were adopted into white families. They were trained to become domestics or stockman, receiving little or no pay (and are still struggling for compensation, in many cases). Children had been told, falsely, that their parents had died, or didn't want them, a source of great confusion in their lives. Sexual abuse occurred. One man told me that he and his sister had been raped by a priest on their first night at the children's home. His sister later developed schizophrenia. I learnt that almost half of the Aboriginal deaths in custody investigated had been stolen children. Sometimes the children who were taken away grew up to be parents who had their children removed, a sad cycle that continues today. I learnt that for many who tried to find their families as adults it was too late. Perhaps the emotional distance between family members was too great, or perhaps the parents they sought had died (the life expectancy of Indigenous people is around twenty years less than our non-Indigenous counterparts).

I was confronted with quotes such as these:

> [Aborigines are] an increasing danger . . . because there are 6000 of the mixed blood growing up it is a danger to have people like that among us.[1]

> If left to their own devices under the present state of the law, their futures will be one of vagabondism and harlotry.[2]

And in the space on a form where the reason for being removed was required, the answer was listed simply: 'for being Aboriginal'.

I was devastated to read, in a letter written by James Isdell, the Aboriginal 'protector' for an area in the north of Western Australia, his philosophy on the removal of children:

> I would not hesitate to separate any half-caste from its aboriginal mother, no matter how frantic her momentary grief might be. They soon forget their offspring.[3]

My research, as well as my commonsense, led me to think that Isdell couldn't have been more wrong. In some traditional communities, after a bereavement the deceased person's name is not spoken again. Indeed other people in the tribe who share that name must change it, to avoid the name being spoken during the grieving period. After a child had been removed, in some communities it was as if the child had died. Those left behind might never see that child again, and so their name was not spoken, and perhaps the child's possessions, or things that were a reminder of that person, were tossed into the sea. This was a ritual for dealing with sorrow, a cultural practice. It had nothing to do with the mother 'forgetting'. Isdell dehumanised the Aboriginal mothers he spoke of. Indeed, Aboriginal people have been repeatedly dehumanised in the 200-plus years since white settlement.

Other stories I was exposed to put hooks into my psyche. I heard of a mother who, having seen her child bundled into the welfare's big, black car without a word said to her, was paralysed with grief and stood in the rain unable to move or speak. That story became the basis of two vignettes in the play for the character of Shirley.

I recall seeing Richard Frankland's film *Who Killed Malcolm Smith* and its gut-wrenching effect on me. From the foyer of the theatre, leaving behind the VIPs in opening-night schmoozing mode, I walked across the road, engulfed by sobs. Frankland's documentary tells the true story of a young Aboriginal boy who 'borrowed' a bicycle from the country bus stop and was punished by geographic and cultural removal. After a lifetime of incarceration he developed a mental illness that culminated in his suicide – he poked a paintbrush through his eye socket into his brain. Even now, writing the words, I am filled with sorrow and anger at the ugliness of a life stolen. Malcolm Smith became the inspiration for my character Jimmy, whose very petty crimes (stealing apples, cans of food) led him down a similar path of removal, institutionalisation and death in custody.

From community members I heard stories of raids by government services and families judged by the contents of their cupboards; this was how it was ascertained whether the parents were 'fit' – by white standards – to raise their children. Antoinette took me on road trips to Cummeragunja, the mission on the Murray, to speak to Elders there about their experiences. And I remember meeting Aunty Iris Lovett, a fabulous, dignified woman who shared with me stories of institutional life: the clinical iron beds with their grey, scratchy blankets; the tin cups; the lack of personal possessions. Her recollections informed the play and were translated into the visual landscape of its first production – a concrete shell with a crack running through it, a filing cabinet and five beds – sensitively designed by Richard Roberts. The beds were a symbol of safety, isolation and institutionalisation, and in Wesley Enoch's production they were moved around the space to heighten the children's anxiety and to highlight their vulnerability to forces beyond their control.

As well as the research materials provided to me by Antoinette, in the six years leading up to the final draft of the play I read every article I could about 'Aboriginal issues' and listened to those who could share their stories. Perhaps, in retrospect, I did lack a little courage, as I felt unable to *directly* ask those people associated with the play who had been removed to share their personal stories with me. It seemed such a painful, traumatic experience. But I was guided by them and by the Ilbijerri committee members who gave me feedback on the scenes that I wrote and that community members workshopped. I felt the weight of responsibility to 'get it right', but I knew also that the members of Ilbijerri would tell me straight if I 'mucked it up'.

My new awareness of the Stolen Generations left me wounded. So how must those who were at the 'sharp end' of those actions feel? What I tried to do in writing *Stolen* was create a work that resonated on an emotional level with an audience. It is important to remember that the work was commissioned by an Indigenous theatre company, not a mainstream one, and its intended audience was Aboriginal people. I did not need to explain the back story – the politics of removal – to Aboriginal people, because they knew it, they'd been there. The brief from Ilbijerri was to tell many stories, not just one, and not to present Indigenous people as a homogenous people who all felt and reacted the same way. As well, they asked that the play not be presented as a straight narrative. What was crucial was to acknowledge the stolen children's suffering and their survival. Having their stories up on stage was a small but significant validation for all they had gone through and continued to go through. The play was not about blame or making a white audience feel guilty. It avoided reference to government policies, as I felt that focusing on those aspects of the story would only divide the audience. It would have been easy to point the finger at governments, churches and non-Indigenous people in general. But would anyone want to listen to that – especially governments, churches and non-Indigenous people? In one UK review the play was criticised for not showing the authorities' point of view. But the play wasn't about that. White people are barely represented. If they want to, they can write their own play, showing their reasons, justifications, the prevalent attitudes of the times and so on. This was a rare opportunity for Koori voices to be heard. And the script was designed to give roles to Koori actors. In a play like *Stolen*, why write roles for white actors?

But I hope I succeeded in my desire that any audience, black or white, could in some way relate to the experience of the characters. In rural Victoria, in a question and answer session after a performance of *Stolen*, a woman stood up and shared how she 'knew how they felt' because it was the first time she had left her small child with a babysitter. She then sat down, embarrassed. I did not in any way belittle her for comparing the act of leaving her child with a babysitter with having your child stolen; rather I was gratified that she had emotionally identified with the characters. Perhaps for the first time Aboriginal people were not 'the other' but mothers – like her – and daughters, sons, real people with real feelings. The memories flood back: a row of 'white' teenage boys openly weeping; a young Aboriginal fella, himself stolen, telling me again and again how the play had inspired him; a text message from a teenage boy in Tasmania (how did he get my number?) blessing me for telling the story. Witnessing the play's effect on the audience was an overwhelming experience.

In speaking about the audience response, I have skipped ahead. In 1997, after the last of the workshops, after six years of development, and with the play finally nearing its final shape, a draft was sent to Playbox theatre. Aubrey Mellor, then artistic director, agreed to program it as a co-production between Ilbijerri and Playbox (now Malthouse Theatre) for their 1998 season. With the talented Wesley Enoch as director, *Stolen* premiered as part of the 1998 Melbourne International Festival. The response was so positive that the season was extended. From that take-off point *Stolen* had a dream run, with eight years of consecutive seasons at the Playbox/Malthouse, thanks in part to its four-year stint on the VCE English syllabus. Over an eight-year period the play also toured most of the east coast of Australia, England (twice), Hong Kong and Japan and had readings in Canada and New York. It was the right play, at the right time. Being dragged along on its coat-tails was an amazing experience for a first-time playwright like myself.

Beyond being the play's writer, my role could have segued into that of 'spokesperson', but I was always careful to emphasise that the things I shared in the question and answer sessions were my opinions, and that I could not speak on behalf of the Stolen Generations. That would have been impudent and disrespectful.

Although as the writer I have not been privy to all the interactions the cast and crew have had with audiences, I have had some interesting experiences when I have been part of the play's entourage. The season at London's Tricycle Theatre in Kilburn was a case in point. The play was chosen as one of four (three Indigenous) plays as part of Heads Up, a season of Australian Arts as part of the Centenary of Federation in 2000. I was fortunate enough to attend the opening night, where VIPs mingled with expats and possibly a small sprinkling of locals! Immediately after the performance, at a gathering upstairs, I observed Peter McGauran, the Minister for the Arts, with tears in his eyes, effusively hugging cast member Glenn Shea. Soon after, a composed McGauran faced the waiting Australian media outside, but if I was hoping for an empathetic address to the media I was disappointed, as he spouted the usual rhetoric, politician-style.

Jill Smith, then general manager of Playbox, has her own memory of the London season:

> [I remember] standing with protesters at a roundabout handing out flyers for the show outside Australia House the night Howard was

having a reception with premiers and past PMs as part of the whole London celebration, of which *Stolen* was a part. The protesters had their 'Say sorry, Howard' banners. Once I had no more flyers I went to the reception!'

Incidentally, the prime minister had been invited to attend the play's opening night. He declined, as he had on previous occasions; I believe on this occasion he attended the tennis instead.

In England the media was certainly more interested in the overall political context in which the play sat, rather than its 'human interest' angle. Indeed, some in the media asked the question no one in Australia was asking, of me at any rate – why hadn't John Howard said 'sorry'? Before the premiere season, Aubrey Mellor had urged me to write a scene that addressed the prime minister's failure to apologise. My response was that I didn't want to give him the air space, and that, anyway, my play was ultimately about the emotional journey of the people who had experienced removal; it was not a play about what I thought would be a temporary political environment (a decade later little has changed). I thought it would be potentially divisive, with half the audience cheering and the other half feeling alienated by its 'political correctness'. The play doesn't seem to suffer from its absence. Mr Howard's refusal hangs in the air like a faint whiff of phenol.

The play's success did have a lot to do with timing, and a great deal to do with the dedication and will of its crew, cast and producers. I can only imagine the effect appearing in the play must have had on the cast members. To work with material that has such significance to the community they represent, and in many cases has a strong resonance in their own lives, must have been amazing. Performing in *Stolen*, I believe, has been a catalyst for healing in their own personal journeys – and mine. I recall travelling to Bourke and Brewarrina after the 2000 Sydney season of *Stolen*, to meet my mother's cousin. She introduced me to an array of relatives, and the family tree I was trying to notate got wider and wider. Although having never met me before, the relatives knew who I was – a descendant of my grandfather, the gun shearer Deucem Smith. My mother's cousin took me out to the cemetery to visit the graves of cousins who had died too young. The most powerful moment for me was when a young black relative greeted me, a stranger, with a grin and 'G'day cuz'. It was a homecoming, to a 'bit a red desert that hadn't seeped into my brain', to bastardise the character Sandy's words, but it felt, somehow, like a place that I had a connection to.

Sometimes it seemed as if life was imitating art imitating life. Tony Briggs, who has since gone on to pen the smash-hit play *The Sapphires*, the story of his mother and aunts' tour in a girl band to Vietnam in the 1960s, played the role of Jimmy in the first season. He had the line 'What do you do when you meet your mother for the first time in twenty-six years?' Not long after his season in *Stolen*, Tony took a trip to the United States, where he met his father for the first time in twenty-six years.

At the end of the play the actors step out of character and address the audience directly about their own lives, a concluding scene conjured by Wesley and the actors during rehearsal for the play's first season. That the actors shared on such a deep, personal level was a precious gift and privilege for audience members, including myself. Indeed it was the most powerful component of the play, the moment where, if they hadn't realised it before, an audience could see, through the lives of these relatively young people on stage, that the Stolen Generations weren't 'in the past', they weren't 'history'. The audience could get some inkling why we couldn't just 'get over it' and 'move on'.

On a more prosaic level, one actor who had performed with the play for a couple of seasons recently thanked me for writing a play that kept so many Aboriginal actors employed for so long.

As for the response of the general public, Playbox took the step of placing a Sorry Book in the theatre foyer, so that audiences could express their responses to the play and to the issue of the Stolen Generations (which had come into focus after the *Bringing Them Home* report was published in 1997). Ironically, the first Sorry Book was stolen. The second version included these entries:

> I don't know how you put yourselves through that in every performance, but I wanted to thank you for doing it.

> Words can't explain the suffering that has occurred and 'Sorry' seems just not enough! This play is the best teaching and help that has been shown to me – keep teaching.

> Having the chance to read and then watch this performance of *Stolen* has opened my eyes to things in Australia's past which are consistently covered over, brushed away, classed as 'too hard'. I appreciate having had this chance and have gained so much. Thanks.

These were responses from the predominantly white audience members. As for black audiences, and I can only go by what blackfellas have conveyed to me personally, the play has meant a validation, an acknowledgment of their experiences of removal.

The critical response to the play was in most cases generous, in some cases very generous. But the most important critique I ever received was when an Aboriginal woman, who was unknown to me, came up to me after a performance. Head down, barely acknowledging me, she said, 'You got it right.' I was deeply moved.

Stolen had an important message to convey, but one play can only do so much to validate, educate and inform, and there is still so much ignorance about the Aboriginal experience post-colonisation. After researching *Stolen*, I realised that nearly all of the social problems faced by Indigenous Australians were connected with the issue of the Stolen Generations. I do believe that the Aboriginal population has been severely traumatised by many of the events of the last 200 years but that our community lives with such a level of trauma that it becomes 'normal'. So many Aboriginal people have experienced the removal of members of their family. Coupled with that the loss of language, separation from their traditional country, endemic racism, institutionalisation and incarceration and the lack of positive role modelling that follows – the list goes on – this becomes 'the way it is'.

If Aboriginal people are living in a state of perpetual trauma, external events relating to the original stress can retrigger the trauma: hence the response by some members of the community to Senator Herron's submission to the Senate inquiry into the Stolen Generation. He said, in an echo of *terra nullius*:

> The actual evidence as to the number of Aboriginal children who were removed is slim . . . At most it might be inferred that up to 10 per cent of children were separated for a variety of reasons, both protective and otherwise, some forcibly and some not. This does not constitute a 'generation' of 'stolen' children. The phrase 'stolen generation' is rhetorical.

How would Senator Herron, the father of ten, have felt if one of his children had been taken? Would there have been a ripple effect across his remaining children? Would the loss have affected generations of his family? Indigenous Australians were, yet again, devastated. Herron's words were 'another stab in the heart', said Carol Kendall, a spokesperson for the National Sorry Day Committee and herself a member of the Stolen Generations. She noted: 'Such denials deeply affected the emotional well-being of those who were taken from their families.' The late Justine Saunders, an Aboriginal actor, handed back her Order of Australia Medal.

After Herron's comments, 250 000 'ordinary caring men and women' walked across the Sydney Harbour Bridge, on an icy May day, in support of reconciliation. In Tasmania, 10 000 walked, in Adelaide, a further 50 000. 'Ordinary' Australians, both black and white, also attended *Stolen*, then touring Sydney, in droves. They wrote deeply felt expressions of condolence in the Sorry Book which travelled with the production of the play. Some audience members – three to date – even had heart attacks, as if they too were suffering from broken hearts.

Yet since then interest in or concern for Indigenous issues, reconciliation and the Stolen Generations has waned. However, there is at least a greater awareness of the issues since the *Bringing Them Home* report and since *Stolen*. As Wesley Enoch wrote in his director's note in the third edition of *Stolen*: 'It is hard to believe now, because it seems that we have always known it, but the general population in the mid-1990s knew nothing about

Aboriginal children being taken away as part of a government policy called Assimilation.' *Stolen* played some small role in the education of, at least, young people. Hopefully awareness brings with it empathy and compassion. These qualities in themselves won't help redress the past, but they will allow an environment in which healing can take place.

So, it is easy to be warmed by or seduced by the success of this play – a total audience of more than 150 000, tours to far-flung corners of the globe, opening nights, awards, but to me its success has always been bittersweet. 'Sweet' because it was developed by an Indigenous theatre group, directed by talented Indigenous directors (to date Wesley Enoch, Rachael Maza, Wayne Blair and David Milroy in their unique productions), has had the benefit of a dedicated and brilliant Indigenous cast, has appealed to audiences and has had critical acclaim. 'Bitter' because it should never have had to have been written. There should have been no reason to tell the plight of children who were stolen from all they knew and all they loved.

The scars linger and it still hurts me to remember those words: 'The mothers soon forget.' They don't.

When

When we live as long as the whitefella, or longer.
When we get hung in the Archibald and not in jails.
When fences can't stop us.
When we don't need our own legal service.
When a form asks if you're <u>not</u> of Aboriginal or Torres Strait Islander descent.
When the 'whites' no longer harm – including the white flour, white sugar, white bread.
When Redfern is an up-market suburb, but nobody's left town.
When there's more of us on a court than before a court.
When the school dropout rate has dropped out of sight.
When our artists get filthy rich, not the dealers.
When the 'blackfella model' is adopted as 'best practice'.
When there's no need for more Royal Commissions.

When you lot can learn to laugh like we do.
When our actors get roles calling for 'doctor, teacher, bank teller' not 'Aboriginal'.
When no one asks 'How *much* of you is Aboriginal'.

Speaking shadows: Justice and the poetic

Gail Jones

(i)

I have always been moved by the story of the poet Paul Celan. A Jew, he was born Paul Antschel in Romania in 1920, and he suffered the loss of both parents in the Holocaust in 1942 and was himself interned in a labour camp until the end of 1943. After the war he moved first to Bucharest, then to Vienna, then finally settled in Paris in 1948, where he became a teacher of German literature at the Ecole Normale Supérieure. He published eleven books of poetry and dozens of translations (including Pessoa, Mandelstam, Rimbaud, Valery and Char), and wrote from a position paradigmatic of much twentieth-century experience: exile, dislocation, a state of permanent mourning. Tormented by unassimilable loss, ruined by desolating sadness, Celan drowned himself in the Seine in his fiftieth year. He crafted his own extinguishment, he opened his mouth to suffocation, he became the hurt, forsaken body his own poetry was seeking.

Poetry did not, alas, save Paul Celan. But against depression, paranoia, breakdown and misery, he maintained a belief in the necessity to write and, indeed, to write *in German*. Celan wished to vouchsafe literary language against historical 'darknesses', to insist on its capacity to hold meaning even against the depredations of fascism:

> Yes, language. In spite of everything, it remained secure against loss. But it still had to go through its own lack of answers, through terrifying silence, through the thousand darknesses of murderous speech. It went through. It gave no words for what was happening, but went through it.[1]

Refusing Adorno's famous dictum 'After Auschwitz to write poetry is barbaric', Celan fashioned poems of astonishing technical virtuosity and moral audacity. They are recondite and often bewildering poems, taut in their metaphysical stringency and challenging abstractions. I first encountered Celan's work as a student, unaware of its complicated context and traditions, and now, years later and much more knowledgeable, I still open a volume of Celan with an expectation of puzzlement. Yet the poetry is oddly companionable in its resistance to easy decipherment: it will not summarise the world; it will not offer facile satisfactions; and it will not admit us comfortably to the netherworld of the poet's experience. It is, in short, beautifully and ethically difficult.

How might such high-literary labour address matters of justice? What might their relation be? And why should one bother with poetic indirection when the horrors of the world are so often blankly and brutally direct? Here is an extract from a poem, 'Speak, you too', which I discovered on my very first encounter:

> Speak –
> But do not separate the no from the yes.
> Give your saying also meaning:
> Give it shadow.
>
> Give it enough shadow,
> Give it as much

As you know to be parcelled out between
Midnight and midday and midnight.

Look around:
See how alive it gets all around –
At death! Alive!
Speaks true, who speaks shadows.[2]

As the poem proceeds, the 'you' of direct address seems to *become* a shadow, becoming thinner, stretching, merging into nothingness. Then air becomes water, and directions of ascent and descent collapse into each other. This is a poem in which the speaking voice and the addressee are in the end unlocatable. Even with all its ambiguity, the poet seems to be recommending an openness of expression and a preoccupation with interstitial forms of knowing, with the struggle to tell the tenebrous uncertainties of history. For Celan, too, Holocaust victims were like shadows because their 'graves' were in the 'sky'; it is the smoky dissolution of humanity to which he returns, again and again, as an image for the anguish that can never be sited and therefore never wholly dealt with.

This wish to pay homage to the 'disappeared' – and in such paradoxical terms – is consistent with imagining the conditions for justice. Knowing the brute and material force of history, Celan nevertheless reminds us of what it is that the poetic can preserve: nuanced interiority, difficult understandings, a sense that the dichotomous forms we are taught to think with are never – *never ever* – the sufficient or efficient basis for a moral life. Speaking shadows is 'thinking with grief', as French philosopher Maurice Blanchot once put it, admitting into our judgment of rights and abuses the informed sorrowfulness of mourning.[3]

(ii)

All nations carry within them events and forms of injustice. There is no equivalence, of course, between specific catastrophes, nor would it be proper to speak of Celan's Holocaust mourning as in any way transferable to Australia. Yet there is some understanding he offers, obliquely and *poetically*, that we might carry to our own country and our own comprehension of 'darknesses'. In April 1997 a report by the Human Rights and Equal Opportunity Commission (HREOC, entitled *Bringing Them Home: Report of the National Inquiry into the Separation of Aboriginal and Torres Strait Islander Children from Their Families*, was tabled in the Australian parliament. It is based on 777 submissions (of which 500 were confidential) inquiring into the forcible removal of thousands of Aboriginal and Torres Strait Islander children from their families. It is a moving and distressing document of the emotional and physical suffering of the people who have become known as the 'Stolen Generations'. Until its tabling few white Australians realised the vast extent of the practice, or indeed the ghastly dimensions of its damage. Apart from frontier violence, the invasion and the expropriation of Aboriginal lands, there was also this lamentable and 'sorry' practice, this decades-long destruction of Indigenous families. It is estimated that 'one in ten' children were removed from their Aboriginal families between approximately 1900 and 1970; the numbers are necessarily vague and the cause of dispute, but, as Robert Manne has pointed out, an exact number is not needed to concede historical wrongdoing.[4]

The testimonies of the 'stolen' are texts of an especial kind, not 'poetic' but straightforward in their manifold grief and often strikingly eloquent in their quality of anguished ineloquence. The testimony is in some ways opposite to the poem: it claims intimate referentiality, a singular, located voice, an immediate and intimate connection between statements and truths. And since the narrative force of testimony in this case can only ever be Indigenous, non-Indigenous writers wishing to engage with 'stolen' matters must write from another perspective and perhaps use forms of indirection that will signal a refusal to 'claim' the experience of others.

Speaking shadows is not just about the admission of mourning into history but also, I believe, about the inclusion of time in one's imagining of other people's sufferings. Just as daylight moves, shifting the visibility of things, so too the wish for justice to prevail is linked with time past and time future, with imagining reparation for wrongs and the instauration of rights. This is the principle of engaged history-writing (such as we see practised by Inga Clendinnen, Henry Reynolds and Anna Haebich, to mention a few); it also works for even the simplest forms of imagining, for one's private memories, and the ways in which we might come to see the ethical failures and achievements within our own lives. Since we live backwards as well as forwards, matters of conscience essentially require this revision; to be self-critical is to be circumspect, to learn what might stand in the way of right or wrong actions and thinking. Writerly elaboration – *naming* the past, speaking of it, offering an account – is one of our forms of negotiation.

Two simple memories travel towards me as I contemplate these matters, both of which come accompanied by a swelling, inner bloom of shame, a sensation of discomfort and moral unease. As a child I lived for several years on the outskirts (five miles away) of the Kimberly town of Broome. This was a multicultural town, of which only about 400 of its population of 1200 were 'white'; most of the community were mixed-race Asian or Aboriginal. Before its touristic expansion in the 1980s it was a town in decline; the once busy pearling industry had subsided and Broome was a sleepy and remote backwater, distinctive, above all, for the racial and ethnic complexity of its population.

In my seventh year, the governor-general visited the town and there was to be a formal welcome and 'presentation' at the small state school I attended. I was chosen to give a speech, and an Aboriginal girl from the Catholic school (the only other school in the town) was chosen to present a bouquet of flowers. We were dressed similarly, each in a stiff flared dress, held by a bow at the back, each with sandals and ribbons in our hair. We marched up the steps of a dais together, and together we curtseyed. There was bunting flapping in the breeze and an Australian flag on the flagpole. I made my little speech and the other girl presented her flowers. We did not speak to each other, nor did I ever learn her name: we were simply wedded in this task of symbolic obeisance to the Crown.

It is difficult now not to see this moment as a corrupt drama of the taken-for-granted privilege of whiteness. The ritual assumed that voice inhered in the white child, and that the task of the Aboriginal girl was to stay silent and hand something over. It is an embarrassing memory because, in a sense, I knew my own pre-eminence, because I too somehow assumed that the possession of words was the possession of value, and that I was the important one, selected to speak.

My second memory is also from my seventh year. A small Indigenous family group 'walked in from the desert'; this was the phrase used in those days to describe the last pre-contact Aboriginal families who were then cautiously entering stations and towns. A boy about fourteen years old, tall, thin, arbitrarily given an English name – I will call him John, just as arbitrarily, since his own tribal name is lost – was placed in my class in school. Too large for the school desks, he sat at a huge packing case at the back of the room, anomalous, lost, speaking no English. With him were three mangy desert dogs, which lay in the doorway of our classroom. Our teacher and the students were all a little afraid of John. Although he slept much of the time, his arms wrapped over his head on the crate, he seemed gigantic among the seven-year-olds and unpredictable in his behaviour. He was given no special teaching, or even attention; he was simply left there, stranded. He sang songs to himself, carved images on the wooden surface of the crate, and laughed at things we did not understand in a voice that was manly. John died in custody in Broome, in his early twenties. I do not know the reason for his imprisonment, or the means of his death, but it seems possible to me that sins of omission – failing to imagine his world and his exile, failing to grant or accommodate his precious otherness – may have contributed to the tragedy of him not finding another life in Broome, of not meeting a future that would make his existence possible.

One wishes one had been a wiser child – asked the name of the silent girl, or befriended the sad, stranded boy from the desert, whose isolation would eventually doom him. The Italian philosopher Giorgio Agamben says that justice is not about repentance, so much as it is about recovering one's own and others' possibilities and potentialities – a kind of dream of plenitude for every life, one that requires imagining backwards (to regret historical mistakes) and forwards (to constitute a more just future).[5] So in these memories of happenstance encounters, I find myself riveted on ideas of time and responsibility. Our experience crucially pre-empts and constitutes us, but it also positions us in forms of address and response, some of which we may not be fully cognisant of until we are adults. An aspiration to justice is an aspiration to full responsiveness to those forms of address that remind us that we exist in 'a community of the question'.[6]

(iii)

It seems to me that there are two challenges here for the writer contemplating issues of justice. The first is that a kind of de-individualising has to occur, something which might seem ill-fitting with the vocation and practice of writing. Ethical and moral laws are not mysteriously inscribed upon the singular heart; they occur in conceptions of public action and in social contracts. Value is in exchange, in dialogue, in complicated forms of reciprocity and redistribution. Much as we might admire what is often described as the individual 'voice' of a writer, it is their participation in cultural value, their more generalised contribution to the richly strange economies of imagination, that finally matters. The necessity of not 'speaking for' others, not assuming the predominance of one's own voice – possibly because it is louder, or more prestigious, or somehow more skilled – is part of this participation. In a multicultural community all voices matter and none should be silenced. Speaking from within a premise of solidarity is of the utmost importance. In an essay, the Nobel prize-winning poet Joseph Brodsky talks of being shown a book of Robert Frost's poems that had been retrieved from STALAG 3B, an Allied prisoner-of-war camp somewhere in France. Across the poem 'Happiness Makes Up in Height What It Lacks in Length' was a size twelve bootprint. Brodsky says the book needed to find its reader, 'Otherwise it couldn't be stepped on, let alone picked up'.[7] The circumstances in which books are 'picked up', taken into another life and self, are trans-individual, historical and perhaps just lucky. In the best of all possible worlds writers may offer forms of circumspection that create the responsiveness at the basis of thinking justly; they may also, of course, simply distract or entertain. Either way, the current cult of personality surrounding writers has little to do with their effects in moral and ethical dimensions, and the claim of being a 'chosen' voice is always already unjust.

The second challenge for the writer is not to succumb to luxurious – that is to say, debilitating – melancholy. Since the contemplation of justice and injustice is a serious matter and likely to lead to despair, there must be a way of entertaining the darknesses that is not pathological but somehow creative and intrinsically resistant.[8] Everyone has heard of Auden's famous slogan (from the poem 'In Memory of W.B. Yeats'): 'Poetry makes nothing happen'; it is cited frequently as a kind of shibboleth of the inefficacy and futility of art. What is often forgotten is the poem's closing line: 'it survives / a way of happening, a mouth'. The speaking of shadows is just this, the mouth that will go on shaping meaning in the face of senseless annihilation. Melancholy is close, too close, to political quiescence: the insistence on affirming commentary, statement, symbol, voice, is fundamental, surely, to imagining otherwise.

(iv)

One of the recommendations of the *Bringing Them Home* report was that the government of Australia might offer a formal apology to the people whose lives were affected by the practices of forced removal. The establishment of 'Sorry Days' was a form of public speech act, as it were, that addressed the wish of many for an acknowledgment – at least – of the necessity of cultural reparation. Hundreds of thousands of Australians signed 'Sorry Books', offering statements of personal regret to be given to Aboriginal leaders, or signed with their bodies in marches of reconciliation. The culmination of this people power was a Sorry Day event on 26 May 2000 in which an estimated 250 000 people marched together across the Sydney Harbour Bridge.

However, the Howard Liberal government famously refused to offer an apology, preferring a triumphalist view of history to one which might admit mistakes; it was also concerned with the cost of possible monetary compensation. Interestingly, in cases in which wronged peoples have been offered money but no apology, as in the relationship between the Japanese government and the Asian 'comfort women' of the Second World War, the compensation is characterised as 'hush money' and leaves the victims feeling trapped in a kind of immoral and destructive narrative. Compensation alone cannot perform the functions of an apology.[9] Those with authority should be rendered 'incapable of approaching the other with empty hands', as the philosopher Emmanuel Levinas memorably put it. He meant that the generosity necessary for justice to prevail is a matter of presenting oneself humbly and apologetically, not just giving over material goods.[10] Refusing even the utterance, the government failed to honour the power of the word to initiate restorative justice, to effect redress for wrongdoing at an initial, symbolic level, and to understand the forms of recognition and affirmation that can occur within words. And it refused, in Agamben's terms, to acknowledge the damage done to the possible futures of others.

My own novel, *Sorry*, was written with some trepidation. It has a political–allegorical aspect – as one would expect, claiming such a title – but it is not centrally concerned with representing the Stolen Generations. As a white Australian, it would be presumptuous to do so and it would risk appropriation of others' painful experience. Nevertheless, *Sorry* deals with culpability and the refusal to say 'sorry', the characteristics, as we now know, of a certain type of (persisting) dispossession. Forgetting, or guilty amnesia, is at the core of the text, yet so too is a loving friendship between an Aboriginal girl and a white girl, one which intimates a kind of ideal of community and reconciliation. Children are both more and less wise than we remember or suppose. The Aboriginal girl is not the 'shadow' of the white girl; rather she is a 'surer presence'. It is also an anti-war novel, concerned with what children witness and the multiplication of levels of violence. In writing such a narrative I rehearsed my own concern that the reconciliation process not be forgotten – since it has certainly faded from the political agenda since the bridge walk of 2000 – and also that the role of language, of what is said and unsaid, must be understood as contributing to the ethical life of individuals and of nations. This sounds a grand claim; in fact it is a modest story, and I know better than to overestimate the role of the 'literary' in political change. It is, more simply, a cautious offering in the process of cultural contrition, and a wish, more personally, to see evident in Australian culture attempts at 'thinking with grief'.

(v)

Paul Celan's most famous poem is 'Todesfuge', 'Death Fugue', written in the late 1940s, not long after the end of the Second World War. It begins like this:

> Black milk of morning we drink you at dusktime
> We drink you at noontime and dawntime we drink you at night
> We drink and drink
> We scoop out a grave in the sky where it's roomy to lie [11]

It is a heartbreaking dirge, an abstracted mourning-song. The graves in the sky, Celan insisted, are not a metaphor: they are an explicit reference to the crematoria at Auschwitz and the reason for this utter reversal of substances and feeling, for this haunting, darkening, pervasiveness of death. 'Todesfuge' was a poem so widely known and anthologised that Celan decided for a time to withdraw if from circulation. It seems he feared its codifying power, the sense in which it perhaps made too explicable something he wanted to remain within the margins of unknowing. Its popularity also made him worry about 'literariness', about the aestheticising of catastrophe. He wrote: 'What matters for language is . . . precision. It does not transfigure, does not "poetize", it names and composes, it tries to measure out the sphere of the given and the possible.'[12] This is an anxiety, I think, for many writers, not just for poets. Although we deal with the symbolic and the metaphoric, although we wish privately, perhaps, to approach the 'beautiful' – whatever that is – we wish too not to ornament indulgently that which is essentially austere. That the signifying of loss might happen through elaborations of language seems a radically interesting conundrum for writing, but not insurmountable in ethical terms. And Adorno's denunciation of poetry was, to do him justice, a kind of warning against the aesthetic refinement and assimilation of barbaric experience.

My response (not resolution) is to return to two metaphors. 'Speaks true who speaks shadows' seems a counter-intuitive position: one is accustomed to the association of light and truth, to the idea of that which is unjustly degraded being 'brought out of the shadows' (a phrase used by Paul Keating in his 1993 Redfern Speech calling for social justice for Aboriginal people). 'Speaking shadows' includes, I think, an admission of uncertainty, a calculation of difficulty, and an awareness that justice – and human relations – is rarely written in black and white. It requires commitment, moreover, to some state of thinking which radically oscillates across time, between past and future, and is therefore a condition of process and hope, rather than of certainty.

The second metaphor I wish to revisit is the bootprint across the poem. This is a profoundly redolent image because it includes both the will to obliterate and the contradicting continuation of the humane. Books and words are less the possession of authors than they are of readers; and it is the reader's 'freedom', not the writer's authority, that finally allows images and narratives their motive force. Celan secretly translated Shakespeare as he worked in the labour camps. This is heart-warming not just because it is so unlikely a story but because it is an act of preservation – indeed extension – of words in the most inhospitable of conditions. The poetic is not some supererogatory expressiveness that is 'unrealistic' or 'out of touch' or committed to hieratic exclusivity: it is part of the resources and pleasure of language and of telling to which every citizen deserves access.

Boring humanist bodies

Adrian Martin

What is it about the name 'Kenny' in Australian cinema? The film that bore this name was the unexpected hit of the local movie scene in 2006; the Kenny of the title (played by Shane Jacobson) is an ordinary guy with a pronounced lisp and a career in portable toilets – a true working-class hero. He's the kind of bloke who hardly seems to have ever left home, let alone the country. But his job puts him into all sorts of social situations – middle-class, upper-class, sporting events, a convention in Japan – that reveal his clumsy but winning naïveté. Actually, in the panorama of Kennys that populate Australian film, this one amounts to a quite benign portrait – you're on his side, and his last word on most incidents is wise and witty. He even gets a girl by the end, and, as one reviewer remarked, the film leaves you 'begging for a sequel'. This particular Kenny's afterlife is already shaping up as a typical media-showbiz phenomenon rather than a big-screen one: awards nights, photo ops, talk shows, race meets, and no doubt a lucrative career as an in-character after-dinner speaker. (But only in Australia: *Kenny* is a parochial film in the most benign sense, unlikely to appeal terribly far beyond our shores.)

Most of the other Kennys of the Australian screen are, however, flat-out deadheads. In *Kenny's Love* (1987), an early short film by Rowan Woods (*The Boys* [1998], *Little Fish* [2005]), the director himself – once better known as a rather ironic comic actor – plays a young man whom many viewers assume to be mentally disabled (although the film itself does not confirm this). He is certainly, to put it politely, childlike. Kenny hangs out at football stadiums selling hot dogs before matches; indeed, his two favourite words, obsessively repeated, are 'footy' and 'doggy' (as in 'hot doggy'). He is maladaptive, a loner, dysfunctional; and Woods seems to look down upon his creation with a mixture of derisive superiority and sentimental indulgence – a two-step we get rather too often in Australian cinema's (predominantly) middle-class portrayals of working-class people. This Kenny really sets the mould of his future namesakes: to mention two other films from 2006, we have the hopelessly manipulated, sexually inadequate, rather stupid Kenny (Anthony Hayes) of Paul Goldman's *Suburban Mayhem*, putty in the hands of the movie's reigning trailer-trash femme fatale (Emily Barclay); and, less centrally, the gormless, obsequious video-documentarist Kenny (played by comedian Tony Martin) of the music-industry satire *BoyTown*, always ready to smile and grovel gratefully for his masters when they give him the merest nod of recognition.

A name; a type; a stereotype. It is useless to rail against the presence of stereotypes in film, especially the kind known as 'popular film' (whether or not the movies in question actually make any money). Their presence is seemingly inevitable – as a handy, shortcut way to picture layers of and relations within a society – and can sometimes galvanise inventive, clever storytelling games. Jeremy Sims's underrated oddity *Last Train to Freo* (2006), for example, showcases a character (played by Steve Le Marquand) who discourses at length to his worried fellow-passengers about the ills of stereotyping a mean-looking suburban guy like him – only to end up, by the time the stage-derived one-act plot has gone through its various convolutions of hidden identity and motive, pretty much confirming the truth of that stereotype. It may be deconstruction at work – the film taking apart its own process of stereotyping from the inside – but it's hard to say.

Unquestionably the rudest, most eye-opening use of Australian stereotypes in recent cinema appeared in a remarkable Korean film partly shot on our shores: Park Chan-wook's *Sympathy for Lady Vengeance* (2005), a lurid, ultra-stylised, queasily 'hypermoral' cap-off to this director's frank Revenge Trilogy. Furiously compressed into hardly four minutes of film-time is every unflattering Kenny-like approximation of the Australian character imaginable: we are infantile (we sleep with our kids, our pets), quite dim (we stare mindlessly at TV's weather channel), imprisoned within walls of infinite sickly-pastel kitsch, boozed and/or stoned out of our minds, and easily frightened and manipulated . . . Did Park derive these stereotypes and clichés from his (possibly whirlwind) observation of our society – or from a crash diet of Australian films from the 1980s and 1990s, particularly those in the *école de Campion*, like *Love Serenade*, *Holy Smoke*, *Soft Fruit* and *Muriel's Wedding*? The most frightening thought is that there may not be much of a difference.

It's hard to imagine a movie as violently zany and as earnestly Nietzschean as *Lady Vengeance* being made by an Australian director. The strong suspicion remains that, even when our filmmakers do manage to put a decent comic spin on such types (as in *Kenny*), it is more a case of the stereotype using the filmmaker, rather than the filmmaker using the stereotype. Something is being regurgitated here, not interrogated: a reflex way of thinking, feeling, reacting – married indivisibly to a conventional way of representing people, depicting events and telling stories. Such, at any rate, was the theme of an argumentative article I wrote all of twenty-three years ago in the magazine *Cinema Papers*: 'A Practical Film Student's Guide to Cliché'. Ostensibly a survey of the student works produced by the various filmmaking/training institutions of the country during the previous year, it worked itself up polemically to a general denunciation of normative cinematic practices at all levels of the industry. A prefatory quotation from a Roland Barthes essay from 1971, proudly titled 'Writers, Intellectuals, Teachers', backed me up:

> Usually the stereotype is a sad affair, since it is constituted by a necrosis of language, a prosthesis brought in to fill a hole in writing. Yet at the

> same time it cannot but occasion a huge burst of laughter: it takes itself seriously, believes itself to be closer to the truth because indifferent to its nature as language. It is at once corny and solemn.[1]

I recall this piece of mine in order to make a historical point. Bitter manifestos decrying the death of Australian cinema have been written by a certain species of critic – the critic beyond the charms of supporting-the-local-industry-at-all-costs jingoism, and keen to place Australian film in an international context, however unflattering that may be – for around three decades now, from roughly the moment that *Picnic at Hanging Rock* overwhelmed many and underwhelmed some in 1975. Every few years these angry pieces explode from a cultural context of exasperation in order to make what is essentially the same argument: that Australian films prize convention over innovation; that we make something less than 'real cinema' – and something more like comfortable bourgeois theatre, mediocre nationalist literature or banal formulaic television.

Such arguments, usually put with great passion, tend to be published in small 'culture magazines' where, more or less, they preach to the already converted and make few waves out in the wider public sphere. They hardly ever count even as passing controversy worthy of a bit of meaningless back-and-forth on talkback radio or in the op-ed pages of our major newspapers. Just recently, in fact, the newer wave of more populist magazines (*Filmink*, *Inside Film* and on the Web *Urban Cinefile*), which have well and truly displaced the older, more serious sort in newsagency racks, have – reverting (by and large) to the jingoistic mode – found a way to demonise virtually all attempts at wholesale critique of Australian cinema: they make out that it is only a few pesky neo-conservative columnists (like Andrew Bolt or Michael Duffy), braying about the immortal 'abuse of taxpayers' money', who are giving bad PR to our worthy filmmaking efforts. If only it were so.

The year 2006 was a strange one for Australian cinema. There were more films being made, released, reviewed and even seen by the public at large than in recent memory; there were a few worthy hits, *Kenny* and (especially) Rolf de Heer's *Ten Canoes* (*BoyTown*, I must confess, has its moments –

especially the daggy dream of Australia's biggest pop band dying in a plane crash before reaching the American Grammys); and a bunch of films were selected for prestigious film festivals overseas (like Cannes and Berlin). And yet, and yet . . . such a high percentage, still, of dissatisfying, deeply flawed or plainly awful films, from *Candy*, *Jindabyne* and *The Book of Revelation* (at the 'artistically ambitious' end) to *2:37*, *Suburban Mayhem*, *Macbeth*, *48 Shades* and *Footy Legends* (at the 'hopeful popular appeal' end). In other words, in short and after all, it was another bad year for Australian cinema – like so many before it.

It often seems that, even when trying to scrape up something to praise, all Australian films hit around about the same mark: *at best*, they are well acted, have a nice sense of place (particularly if it's a rural, small-town or seaside place), have lovely photography and a pleasant music score . . . But most of these films, of the *Caterpillar Wish* variety, are ones you (or, at any rate, I) would never want to see twice. This is what I think of as the 'Australian cinema at 4 am' syndrome: those (many) local films which unfailingly end up programmed solely in the wee hours of free-to-air and cable television networks.

Australian cinema is very prone to filmmaking clichés that whip through the system like a virus – eagerly taken up, it seems, by producers, writers and directors with an eye on the talked-up 'latest thing' in world cinema, and an ear on whatever is being pushed in the various government-run project-development labs. On the one hand, for instance, we have the baleful influence of the 'Mike Leigh effect': local workshops reverently transmit to the colony this British director's semi-improvised process for building characters in collaboration with the actors – resulting in appallingly static screen characterisations where a bunch of broadly brushed 'tics' are repeated *ad nauseam*. (*Little Fish* is an example, as is Cherie Nowlan's *Clubland* – and, lo and behold, we are back with the hyperreal working-class portraits). On the other hand, we see a briefly popular technique quickly codified and exhausted: films structured around or punctuated by mock interviews with the characters (as in *2:37* and *Suburban Mayhem*) – a poor, clumsy substitute for inventive narrative exposition and character exploration – in which, with thudding obviousness, people either lie through their teeth (as they nervously avert their eyes) or break down and tell all.

But the reigning arguments over 'what is wrong with Australian cinema' are now in a stalemate. Not only is nobody 'out there' listening or making urgent moves to reform the system but even those who utter these polemics no longer really believe the terms of their once-fiery critique. A weariness has set in, because mainstream Australian cinema, on the whole, never changes – and the alternatives to it find themselves more marginalised than ever, as much a victim of their own rhetoric as of the insular, defensive mechanisms of the filmmaking 'establishment'.

It is salutary, facing such a bind, to work back through the annals of Australian film criticism and theory, precisely in order to ask two questions: Where did the critique go off track? Why did it lose its shot at being an effective agent of change?

But first, a word on the impetus for this essay – an invitation to write about film in the context of 'writing and justice'. That initial guideline referred, of course, mainly to literature, but the editor may not have realised the particular resonance which the word 'writing' carries in the history of film theory and criticism. Back in the 1960s and 1970s, and intermittently thereafter, writing was a fighting, radical term – a translation and transposition of the French *écriture*, associated with the big guns of Barthes and Jacques Derrida. In this appropriation, 'writing in film', or even writing a film, did not mean what it (commonsensically) sounds like: it had nothing to do with scriptwriting, with words on a page. Rather, *écriture* signified everything that was truly *cinematic* in film: the writing that occurred with what Alexandre Astruc called, back in the 1940s, a 'camera-pen', with the material work of images, sounds, colours, rhythms, performance gestures: cinematic *style*, if we agree to elevate rather than debase this word.

A now-mythic critic, Serge Daney, who was in the 1970s and 1980s an editor of the world's most famous film magazine, *Les Cahiers du cinéma*, once put the veritable mystique of this approach to film in a nutshell: 'It's quite simple: the cinema loved by the *Cahiers*, from the beginning, is a *cinema haunted by writing*.'[2] And writing – even to the point of what

Daney calls an 'excess of writing' – is set against *ideology*: the determination of everything in a movie by good intentions, noble themes, socially symbolic characters . . . (And when all three of those come together, the end-result is *overdetermined*, as in the clumsy 'racial reconciliation' ending of *Jindabyne*.) For Daney, writing – good writing, at any rate, by the best filmmakers – is accompanied by something else that sounds more natural in French than it does in English: an *exigency*, an exacting and highly moral point of view. A good, valuable film for Daney is rigorous, difficult, hard to 'claim' for one ideological agenda or another. Its writing reveals, step by step, the traces of the relationship between the mind of the filmmaker and the material – both of previous cinema and of the real world – that he or she is grappling with. Cinema, for Daney, is the attempt – always doomed, frequently heroic – to represent, to express, to *figure* (another, more recent term favoured by French critics). And filmic writing – the setting-in-place of each image and sound in relation to those surrounding it – is the dramatisation of this struggle. To return to the theme of this collection, I find myself phrasing it thus: *to what must* (filmic) *writing do justice*? To 'the real', of course – Daney always asserted that 'cinephilia is not just a special relationship to cinema; it is a relationship to the world through cinema'[3] – but also to the possibilities of film as style-in-action, as thinking in and through the materials of the medium.

For many years the harshest critics of Australian film – at least those in the writers–intellectuals–teachers category – have argued that our cinema is too hung up on *content* (well-rounded characters, well-constructed and believable stories) to the utter detriment of *form* (which is another, plainer way of translating *écriture*). It's an argument which is hard to pose convincingly in the daily papers, where it runs up against the simple fact that the vast majority of ordinary filmgoers shell out their money for interesting characters and good stories. This does not invalidate the position in favour of form, or 'writing'; rather, it indicates that, while its effects are powerful and pervasive – in fact completely constitutive of the film as a living, breathing object, as in every other aesthetic medium – form passes under the radar of most filmgoers' conscious minds. This is what is so grating about those how-to-write-a-script gurus regularly flown out by our government organisations devoted to the development and funding of film: the nonsense they preach about 'the story being all' (not to mention 'characters you can identify with') plays right along with the lowest common denominator of the film-viewing experience, rather than its highest possibility. But what can be expected of a country in which a major 'public intellectual' like playwright David Williamson seriously proposes the following as a program of literary education?

> Perhaps the simplest solution to the culture war posturing would be to have two separate areas of study. Rhetoric, which examines the way words manipulate, and story, which would allow access to the accumulated wisdom of great works and filmmakers, past and contemporary.[4]

There we have the saddest binary opposition of them all: form equals rhetoric equals manipulation equals lies, while story (Williamson here adopting directly Hollywood's screenwriting lingo) equals the highbrow wisdom of the ages. (His one touch of modernity is galling: just add film!) Yet how does one shrug off this depressingly massive load of dreary commonsense? (Definition of a critic: the one who doesn't stand for commonsense.) In the case of film critics down the past thirty years, the touting of form against 'mere' content quickly led to the scapegoating of a particular villain: *realism*. Workers in this particular milieu have often read (in long-defunct magazines like the Sydney Filmmakers Co-Operative's *Filmnews*, or academic journals such as *The Australian Journal of Screen Theory*, *Continuum* and *The UTS Review*, as well as a spray of art catalogues and essays on literature or performance) that, in movies of all stripes, the 'real', the 'natural', the 'true' (all those frightening commonsense words eternally deserving of scare-quotes) were all just horrid alibis for what one commentator called the 'nasty social relations' of the status quo. Realist film – and, in the polemics of the time, that covered most film with stories, characters and a more-or-less consistent fictional world – regurgitated (and hence justified, reinforced) the world as it was, as it is, as it ever will be, as defined by a specious 'universal humanity'. People are as they are, all too human, and art (apparently) proves it to us: the conservative culture-monger is the one who always thinks that he or she has seen and understood it all before, in the 'accumulated wisdom of great works' by Shakespeare, Dostoevsky, et al. How different this is from the position of Daney who believed that, in the drama of cinematic writing, there has to arise 'an affirmation of something new to think'.

But where does the virulent rejection of realism lead? To a militant non-realism: the embrace of complex, artificial, highly self-conscious forms, deliberately short on narrative and characterisation, high on 'writing'. The postmodern film, the layer-upon-layer film (movies about the making of movies), the essay-film: a generation or two of smart independent film-makers in Australia, led also by their political passions in left, feminist, Indigenous and gay movements, embraced these tricksy formats, sometimes with disastrous results. The feature films in this mode that managed to be funded and made, from Gillian Leahy's *My Life Without Steve* (1986) and David Perry's *The Refracting Glasses* (1992) to Tracey Moffat's *Bedevil* (1993) and John Hughes's *What I Have Written* (1995), testify to the highwire risks of the anti-realist stance: sometimes thrilling experiments, too often short-circuiting contraptions. The palpable suspicion of a certain, conventional kind of coherent, singular narrative – as a lure, a trap, a prison – ends up becoming wearisome and self-defeating. Britain's Ken Loach, once the most pilloried of 'unreflective realists', has outlived (as an artist, and also at the Australian box office) this entire independent-cinema movement, and it will be worth asking, in a little while, just why this might be.

Today, there is a less politicised, more 'populist' mutation of the 'argument for form' in Australian cinema. It consists of proselytising for *genre* cinema in all its shapes and modes: slick and expensive (like the films of Michael Mann and Martin Scorsese) or cheap and rough (the rich history of 'B', exploitation and underground movies). The cry goes up: why don't our middlebrow funding bodies break rank and get behind the production of horror films, action movies, sex comedies (like in the good old

Bazza Mackenzie days), sci-fi fantasies? Such a shift – so the argument goes – would instantly create an upturn in 'cinematic thrill': the stuff of colour, pace, spectacle that all true film fans crave. Yet the examples that exist of this policy in practice, from *Sensitive New Age Killer* (2000) and *Undead* (2003) to *Suburban Mayhem* and *Macbeth*, reveal a sad contrary truth: an orgy of explosive effects with no sustaining, underlying ideas – beyond, that is, the most obvious tabloid-type ideas, such as 'alienation rules suburbia', 'absolute power corrupts absolutely' or 'families are funny things'. When a fan-boy special like *Undead* enjoys the spectacle of rounding up aliens in compounds and exterminating them, without the slightest sense that this resonates (disturbingly) with present-day political situations in Australia, it is a sure sign that the pro-genre position needs rather more work to be a viable progressive alternative.

The critique of Australian cinema finds its echoes in many countries, at many times, in many cultural contexts, and it is instructive to examine how these neighbouring polemics have played themselves out. Almost ten years ago, for instance, the progressive 'little magazine' *Balthazar*, published by a group of young French film students who are now the cutting-edge critics among the *Cahiers* staff, ran a stirring polemic (by Mathias Lavin and Stéphane Delorme) against what the mass media of the time (and still) extolled as the 'Young French Cinema': a group of largely academic film-makers making clean, well-acted, well-meaning dramas, often on a topical social theme like AIDS or the plight of illegal immigrants (in Australian art-house cinemas, we know this French tendency best via the work of François Ozon). Much of this attack uncannily echoes the terms of the Australian debate, before and since: the target is those films that aim to merely 'tell a story, love their characters, dispense a civic duty, etc', rather than 'criticise or displace the mass neo-classicism that occupies every screen on the planet'. And the description of a 'character-driven' cinema (how often one hears this dreaded term in Australian script-development workshops!) encapsulates the too-modest ambition and scope of so many of our family-centred movies:

> Scenes of daily life. The scenario is always the same: anecdotal. The subject is never the human (in its eventual relation to the animal, the vegetable, the mineral, the machine), only the individual – defined, characterised, assigned. We are immediately in a reduced social theatre, where psychology is king. How many filmmakers manage to extricate themselves from the psycho-social in order to accede to a broader (anthropological, aesthetic) viewpoint? Me, me, me, little me . . . There's the sole-me, the group-me and the family-me.[5]

In part, the *Balthazar* piece is, yet again, an anti-realist polemic (realism being the pervasive curse which, according to these young Turks, implicates even the founding fathers of critique, André Bazin and Daney): the 'cinema of moral dignity', they write, 'risks falling into artistic nullity' if it insists upon the simplistic notion that film is a 'transparent recording of reality' rather than a 'figurative laboratory'. In Australia cinema today, 'transparency' is not really, any more, the problem – if, indeed, it ever was. Do the makers of *Razzle Dazzle*, *Clubland* or *BoyTown* believe they are 'recording reality'? Of course not. Even the most conventional of filmmakers consciously inhabit one or other stylised world that suits the mood and pitch of their project: whimsical small-town vignette, gaudy showbiz milieu, parodic take on movie or television formulae, etc. But that figurative laboratory is indeed an inspired, and urgently relevant, concept – an idea with legs, an 'affirmation of something new to think'.

There is one particular element in this laboratory that I want to take up here. It is the idea of character, the performance of character in film – not in the realm where 'psychology is king', but neither in the anti-realist realm where character is abolished altogether in favour of the emblematic ciphers that corrode many local films of high ambition. The *Balthazar* editors – having criticised the tendency of the Young French Cinema films to produce characters who are completely 'readable', instantly recognisable in their gestures, able to be mapped onto a completely conventional code of anger, love, melancholy and so on – conclude: 'There is no work on the body as created or devoured by the image, no invention of another way of acting, another diction, another corporeality.' In other words, a cinema of *boring humanist bodies*, flatly filmed, predictably 'three dimensional', merely representative of something or other, walking-talking platitudes. They could just as easily be talking about *Candy*, *Book of Revelation* or *2:37*, films which, from end to end, lazily recycle the most banal and egregious clichés of how to express, in the language of their medium, extreme emotional states of patly 'divided' characters: spinning overhead shots of prone bodies to signify angst, 'frolic' scenes to convey joy, punch-in of a folky song (preferably by Paul Kelly) over shots of pensive faces for a reflective montage sequence.

Instead of blasting off at this point into the unrealist or highly artificial spheres of fantasy-horror, animation or avant-garde abstraction, we can stay with actors, stories, fictive worlds: the basic coinage of mainstream cinema. In fact, let us alight, in passing, upon a model too often misidentified as the very height or acme of realism in cinema: the intense, even melodramatic, intimate dramas of John Cassavetes in America and Maurice Pialat in France, running from the early 1960s through to the mid 1990s. (Since then, the tradition has been continued at its apex by Abel Ferrara in America, the Dardenne brothers in Belgium, and – let's admit it at last – Ken Loach in Britain.) We can already see, along this sorry line of misidentification, an appropriation of such a tradition in Australian cinema: the partly or entirely improvised films like Kriv Stenders' *Blacktown* (2005) and Scott Ryan's *The Magician* (2005), spurred on more immediately by the much-publicised 'Dogma Manifesto' of Lars von Trier and his Danish associates, which are freewheeling 'in the moment' pieces, shot (with many excess hours left over in editing) on digital cameras. These frequently shapeless films – and there are many more of the kind on the way – may think they are tapping a vein of dramatic 'kitchen sink' authenticity through spontaneity, but they, too, quickly fall into their own cauldron of tried and untrue psychodrama clichés: characters are forever telling elaborate lies, tearing off each other's public masks and having confrontations and teary breakdowns . . . But such histrionic devices do, alas, fit all too well with the Mike Leigh *Secrets and Lies* model of 'exacerbated naturalist' acting and dramaturgy.

Cassavetes and Pialat had nothing to do with such naïve filmmaking practices (nor, by the way, did they actually improvise very much, or indulge shaky hand-held camera work as an ironclad stylistic rule). The contemporary French critic/theorist Nicole Brenez, discussing Cassavetes' *A Woman under the Influence* (1974), brilliantly intuited the deepest artistic process of this cinematic tradition: within the strictly circumscribed, defiantly low-budget space of domestic drama (one house, a few characters), beginning from the old familiar themes of romantic love and family ties, nonetheless 'certain very simple acts remain absolutely incomprehensible', while, 'inversely, certain very difficult, delicate phenomena, among the oldest in the history of representation, are treated in a resolutely clear manner'. A look at Cassavetes' films clarifies this mind-boggling concept instantly: when characters meet and collide, often in a highly charged atmosphere, we usually have no immediate idea who they are to each other (siblings? friends? intimates? strangers?), whereas incredibly complex states of being (Brenez lists 'madness, brotherhood, performance', and there are many more) are concretised in unforgettable gestures of a hand, a mouth, an unforeseen bodily posture . . .

In a very real sense, what Brenez is invoking here is the avoidance or refusal of stereotype and cliché – or, more precisely, the twisting so completely of what is familiar that it comes out resembling nothing but itself, a singularity. In the films of Cassavetes and Pialat, this avoidance or transformation of the cliché – which seems to be the deepest wellspring of their creativity – affects every level of the filmmaking process: the shaping of the storyline, the staging of scenes, the direction of actors. Again and again, a dramatic or comic situation we have seen a thousand times before – seen so often we have forgotten it, overlooked its ossification into the purest cliché – explodes before our eyes and ears in a new way, 'diverted' into a new meaning, a new spectacle. A person arriving home from work, someone receiving tragic news at their front door or over the telephone, a woman telling her lover that she is pregnant . . . Such events are switched around, told from a new perspective, perhaps boldly elided altogether (Pialat's speciality).

Rather than having state-sponsored seminars on the 'hero's journey' and the reassuring mythic grandeur of 'story', or primers on the formulae of populist genres, wouldn't this be a better way to train and develop Australian filmmakers: to ferret out, with a truly critical vigilance, every cliché in advance (they will always creep in, let's face it), and then to set about inventing ways – the cleverest, the fondest, the most profound ways – of transforming them? Australian cinema, certainly, would then no longer be so damnably, predictably 'corny and solemn'.

Such work, which begins from the most basic elements of a film project – where to take the story next, how to convey the detail in a scene, where to position the players – can take us into the most complex and delightful aspects of cinema as a figurative laboratory. Consider, for example, *Balthazar* magazine's call for 'work on the body as created or devoured by the image', and thus the 'invention of another way of acting, another diction, another corporeality'. One logical place to explore the creation of such bodies is, indeed, in those unreal populist genres that literally allow such extravagance: horror, fantasy, sci-fi. But it takes more than simply writing a zombie, alien, vampire or fairy-tale apparition into a script to kick the figurative laboratory into gear. We catch glimpses of 'other corporealities' from time to time in Australian cinema – in the ghostly villains of *Wolf Creek* (2005) and *The Proposition* (2005), or the inexplicable, frightening visions of unidentified, menaced bodies in short avant-garde pieces like James Clayden's *The Desealer* (2006) and Corrie Jones' *Victim* (2003).

But even the presence of a perfectly inert, dead body – in a relatively realistic thriller or drama – can set the figurative wheels spinning: filmmakers from Alfred Hitchcock (in *Psycho*, 1960) to Brian De Palma (*The Black Dahlia*, 2006) have realised that to place a corpse at the centre of a movie is to introduce a contagion of the uncanny, of shades of existence between the living and the dead, that end up powerfully contaminating and transgressing all the hitherto established characters, values, themes and social structures. But can we say the same of the ever-floating, watery corpse in *Jindabyne*? Even in death it is a boring humanist body – merely the sign of a life that has been snuffed out – which unhinges nothing but a few perturbed moral consciences in characters' heads. Robert Altman, who used the same Raymond Carver story as the basis for a thread in *Short Cuts* (1993), knew what to do with this body, how to show the everyday kind of horror it unleashes: you watch the guys on their fishing trip pissing on it. Ray Lawrence's film, however, has neither this courage nor this conviction: its dose of 'otherness' (handily condensed in the hammy body of Chris Haywood's serial killer) is left roaming the outskirts of town, while the spirit of the dead Indigenous girl is simply laid to rest or set free, New Age style, in a ceremony of community healing set to the inevitable Paul Kelly ditty . . .

I wonder again: to what must filmic writing do justice? To itself – to its highest possibilities as expression, entertainment and art – and to the spectator, too, no longer treated as the automatic 'reader' or passive receiver of every long-cemented cliché. And thus to the reality – all the tough, burning issues of contemporary Australian reality – that can never be simply reproduced, signalled, gestured to, or even dramatised in some neat allegory or satire (which is the particular curse bequeathed by contemporary Australian mainstream theatre).

'Images unify', warned Daney, 'through common fear or recognition', while 'writing divides',[6] making reality hard to identify, difficult to consign, impossible to consume. The surprise or shock of non-recognition, produced through a truly canny, witty, erudite work of filmmaking, leads to new thoughts, unexpected debates . . . and possible futures.

Aboriginal children's literature: More than just pretty pictures

Anita Heiss

There is far more to Aboriginal-authored children's books than telling the expected Dreaming or creation stories through 'just words' and brightly coloured artwork. Rather, in recent years books in this genre have raised the bar in terms of this literature's cultural worth, with Aboriginal titles being increasingly defined by their social, cultural, historical and political value. Many titles coming out of Indigenous-specific publishing houses, like Magabala Books in Broome and IAD Press in Alice Springs, serve to define and demonstrate the roles and responsibilities of Aboriginal children's literature. These books explore aspects of Australian history and society not regularly covered in other areas of Australian children's book publishing or in the education system. Stories about Aboriginal identity written by young Aboriginal authors, books that provide young readers with moral lessons, and stories that not only entertain and engage young readers but also carry the cultural role of documenting language are increasingly highlighting the difference between mainstream children's books, which may have entertainment value but no determination or responsibility to provide role-model characters or storylines with a greater social purpose, and those written by Aboriginal people. I want to explore here how some of these Aboriginal-authored titles, which use local and personal histories, including complex stories that deal with the Stolen Generations, engage and educate young readers.

The traditional story time in infant schools remains an important part of the Australian educational curriculum. A strategic way to introduce young Australians – black and white – to aspects of Aboriginal society they may not get anywhere else is to engage a captive young audience with a well-written and enthusiastically read page-turning story, with colourful illustrations. It is important to note at the outset, however, that these books have a broad-ranging audience. Readers interested in Indigenous stories, culture, language and voice are not limited by age, gender, class or geography. One obvious example of a book that appeals to a wide audience is the beautifully designed and presented *Papunya School Book of Country and History* (2001), a text that has increased greatly the understanding and appreciation of the cultural value of Aboriginal-authored children's books.

Papunya School Book of Country and History was made by Anangu staff and students at the Papunya School in collaboration with children's author Nadia Wheatley and illustrator Ken Searle. The book was developed as part of the school's curriculum resources, and went on to win the 2002 CBC Eve Pownall award and was Joint Winner (with *Go Facts Animals, Plants and Oceans*) of the Australian Book Publishing 2002 Award for Excellence in Educational Publishing. The judges of the latter commented:

> The clarity and structure of the writing in *Papunya* provides, to readers of all ages, access to a very complex and complicated part of Australia's history. Developed as a collaborative project between staff, students and the authors, Papunya has cross-curriculum applicability. Its holistic and innovative approach to learning helps teachers and students to achieve a range of outcomes through study of the lives of the first Australians.[1]

The development process of the book at times involved as many as a dozen people producing one picture, while the text was checked and re-checked by staff, and an earlier version of the book was trialled in the classrooms. The process of consultation between the community and those enlisted to assist the production process (Searle and Wheatley) demonstrates the culturally appropriate way in which this publication was developed, a method that has ensured that the most accurate, informative and valuable book went to the printer.

While Indigenous control of projects is important, collaborations between communities and those who have particular industry skills (such as writing and painting for publication) are essential in ensuring that Aboriginal stories are prepared for maximal audience exposure. The Australia Council guide, *Writing Cultures: Protocols for Producing Indigenous Australian Literature*, lists 'communication, consultation and consent' as integral to producing the best Aboriginal literature possible. Importantly, even with such collaborations, copyright should rest with the Aboriginal individuals or organisations. In this case it rests with the Papunya School.

The *Papunya School Book of Country and History* is not just for kids. The book crosses many genres, including non-fiction and biography, and is an attractive coffee-table art book. It is possibly also a 'bible' of sorts for the community that lies 200 kilometres west of Alice Springs, where the Anangu (the Aboriginal people of the central desert region) are the traditional owners of the land, and where English and Luritja are spoken at school, and the languages of many countries are spoken at home.

As a book of social importance, it contributes to improved understanding between Aboriginal and non-Aboriginal Australians, but the work also functions as a history book and was applauded as such when it won the 2002 NSW Premier's Young People's History Prize. The judges remarked on the book's historical significance:

> *The Papunya Book of Country and History* is a remarkable and long overdue departure from the traditional model of history writing for young people. It offers not one voice but many, not one story but several, it builds a living bridge between ages and across cultures. This is a book that recognises the importance of both the visual

> and the written narrative in capturing young people's interest in their past; its stories and images are vivid and captivating, enriching and challenging. It offers non-Indigenous Australians (of all ages) a chance to learn from Aboriginal culture and empowers Anangu people through the recovery of both shared and divergent stories. Indeed, *Papunya* is a salutary example of 'shared authority' in the writing of history and demonstrates the educational imperatives of the reconciliation process. This book is a powerful statement about our country's past and a signpost to a better future.[2]

In light of these comments, it is easy to see that the audience for this book is not simply the children of the school but the community as a whole and a broader Australian readership that now has the ability to learn about a particularly rich region of Australia. Tens of thousands of Australian and international tourists enjoyed the visual delights of the 'Papunya Tula: Genesis and Genius' exhibition at the Art Gallery of New South Wales in 2000. The first of its kind to trace the phenomenon of the Papunya Tula movement from the early 1970s to the present, this exhibition was part of the Gallery's contribution to the Sydney 2000 Olympic Arts Festival, and was curated by Hetti Perkins. But how many of those gallery visitors, before they went and after, would have understood the history behind the peoples who produced those amazing works? In her review of the exhibition, Susan Allen applauded it as 'a valuable overview of some of the most important work by Aboriginal artists from Australia's Western Desert'.[3] However, she also commented that the exhibition and accompanying catalogue of essays 'made no attempt to explore the complex aesthetic and political questions posed by the emergence of Papunya Tula and the rapid growth of contemporary Aboriginal art'.[4] The catalogue records in book form the Papunya Tula movement from the early 1970s to the present. In contrast, *The Papunya School Book of Country and History* discusses the renowned artwork, inclusive of the people, the country, the history and the Tjukurrpa yard (Dreaming stories) of the area from the 1850s to the present.

This multi-genre book is a compilation of drawings, paintings (including dot paintings) and timeline and information boxes, and provides a comprehensive understanding of the history of Papunya since the first Tjulkura (white people) appeared in their *ngurra* (country) and the local people feared them as *mamu* (ghosts or devils). The reader travels visually through generations of stolen land, the killing of stock, Anangu resistance and the arrival of white explorers right through to the arrival of missionaries and the gospel and 'devils in the sky' (aeroplanes), the first school in Papunya in 1960, and onto the 1992 High Court decision on native title which led to the handing back of a sacred site of Pulka Karrinyarra (what whitefellas call Mt Wedge) in July 1999. These are all significant moments in the history of Papunya, and it is the simplicity of the book that makes such complex issues and events so accessible to all ages and literacy levels.

In the section 'A New Way to Paint Country', we learn in one paragraph about how Arrente man Albert Namatjira began painting landscapes, while Mary Malbunka's painted map gives an aerial view of how Haasts Bluff looked when she was a five-year-old child, and offers a simplistic understanding of where the school lay in relation to the 'ration place', 'the whitefella's house', the church, the water tank and the road to Alice Springs. The timelines offer simple yet significant notes on what happened and when in the region and nationally.

The Papunya School Book of Country and History has proved to be overwhelmingly popular with readers and teachers; the title is carried in hundreds of libraries nationally (local, school and university) and teachers notes have been developed for use in the classroom with students of 'all ages'.

Reading about the history of Australia has never been so interesting and enjoyable, although schoolchildren often claim that learning history is boring. Teaching resources are the key to teaching history in an engaging way and the template designed by Papunya School could easily be adapted by communities nationally, both Aboriginal and non-Aboriginal, as a means of recording the history of a particular place and people, making it interesting and relevant to children around the country.

Following that template is the late Mary Malbunka's *When I Was Little Like You* (2003), which shows the similarities between children growing up, regardless of where they live and their cultural affiliations. Malbunka's strategy is one of unifying children of different backgrounds, in contrast to the fear of difference that is often instilled by mainstream media. The author uses language (her own Luritja and English) as well as contemporary illustrations and traditional dot paintings to tell the story of her life as a *pipirri* (child) growing up in both her mother's *ngurra* (country) and her father's *ngurra* – Warlpiri and Pintupi.

When one reads of her childhood, it is obvious why Malbunka has chosen the inclusive title *When I Was Little, Like You*. There are some things that *all* young people do regardless of culture, social status or geography, such as playing games, swimming (whether beach, river or creek), building and playing in cubbyhouses, ditching school, knocking off fruit from the neighbour's tree and garden and so on. These are things I also did as a young child growing up in the eastern suburbs of Sydney. Of course, there were things that Malbunka did as a child that I didn't do, although I wished I had – like sitting around the campfire and learning from the old people about placenames and stories relevant to nearby lands. While I didn't learn that way, Malbunka's book shows me how she did, and how she later passed that same information on to young people in her country: information like where some animals are found; for example, the *tjilkamata* (echidna) and *kanyala* (wallaby) prefer *puli* (rocky country), while the *malu* (kangaroo) and *kalaya* (emu) can be found in *jjata* (scrub country). We also learn that it's best to hunt for *malu* in the dry season because that's when they are the fattest.

Although this book is classified in the genre of children's and youth literature, it will engage readers of all ages, page after page. The language notes and diagrams at the end of the book assist the reader to understand how to read Malbunka's illustrations and thus make the most of this culturally and socially rich book.

Like *The Papunya School Book*, Mary Malbunka's work is also a history book for all Australians. It was shortlisted for the 2003 NSW Premier's History Award for Young People, and the judges commented:

> This clearly told story would appeal to both Aboriginal and non-Aboriginal children, with its narratives of Mary's life, growing up in the 1960s. Historical elements include experiences at a government settlement, glimpses of traditional living, 'Sorry Business' and difficulties of dealing with the demands of two languages – English and Luritja. Both languages feature in the story-telling with an English/Luritja glossary provided. An appealing book, it is an interesting recording and passing on of experiences closely resembling traditional oral accounts. It plays an important role in furthering cross-cultural understandings and empathy amongst Australian children.[5]

Jackie Huggins, Co-Chair for Reconciliation Australia, wrote: 'This beautiful work is a gift to children, education and reconciliation.'[6] And so it is.

One young reader highlighted the value of this title in educating other young readers about Aboriginal Australia, the consequences of invasion and the process of colonisation. Eleven-year-old Alice from Adelaide wrote:

> I really thought that the illustrations in the book were excellent and I like the style in which they were drawn. The colours that were used were really good and made me feel like I was in the outback. I also liked the dot paintings that were in the book. I liked the way the book taught me about traditional aboriginal culture and lifestyle – like the hunting, tracking, exploring and playing that went on. I liked the way they learned things from the stories their families told them. I think it also gives you an idea of how the Aboriginal people's lifestyle has been affected by the white man's world.[7]

The basic foundation for any form of reconciliation to work in Australia is understanding; whitefellas need to understand fully their own history, that is, the shared history of this country post-1788 and the impact that white Australia has had on black Australia since first contact. With that understanding comes empathy and a desire to learn more about the cultures and societies of the First Peoples of Australia. Such learning begins with books like Mary Malbunka's, laying the foundation for understanding with young people in the classroom and the local library. It begins by placing them in Malbunka's shoes, in her country when she was a child growing up, and then relating that experience in some way to their own life experiences today.

Other elements of history considered in Aboriginal picture books include titles that deal with the Stolen Generations and the forced removal of Aboriginal children as part of the government's policies of protection and assimilation. While many adult Australians are now more aware of the history behind, and the continuing repercussions of, the Stolen Generations, many of them have not read the important 689-page volume *Bringing Them Home*, which is the report from the National Inquiry into the Removal of Aboriginal and Torres Strait Islander Children from Their Families. While Australians may be interested in this aspect of their shared history, they still need material presented to them that is palatable, not *too* confrontational or challenging, and accessible in literary terms. For children, resources on such serious issues need to be in a format that will not traumatise them, like the young Aboriginal people who were removed in the past were traumatised. But how does one tell such a terrible story to young children, both black and white?

One example is *Down the Hole: Up the Tree, across the Sandhills . . . Running from the State and Daisy Bates* (2000), a true story of the 'The State People' stealing children, 'just kidnapping them' as part of the policy of 'Protection' in South Australia.[8] *Down the Hole* is a children's book that takes very complex aspects of history and politics and translates them, simplifying them for both children and adults so that they can understand them, relate to them and engage with them.

The story tells of Edna Tantjingu Williams, originally from Tarcoola, and Eileen Wani Wingfield of Ingomar Station, and the experiences they had as children avoiding the dreaded 'State People' who visited Coober Pedy where the girls grew up. We read of children hiding in bushes and the extraordinary lengths to which parents went to ensure that their children weren't taken, such as putting them down holes in the ground then sending food down by rope:

> My old people used to chuck us down pitingka – chuck us down the holes . . . We used to sit down real *quiet* too . . . And the poor Old People used to look around everywhere before they can send a feed down, you know.[9]

The memory recall in this story is not laden with terror or even bitterness, so that rather than young readers being afraid or scared of the storyline, it is likely they will be concerned about why young Aboriginal children had a life so different from their own today.

Such desperate measures on the part of parents, behaviour that today would never be necessary or acceptable, will have young readers asking, 'Why did the kids have to hide? Why did the government want to take the Aboriginal kids away?'.

Both teachers and parents will be expected to be able to respond to such enquiries as sensitively as the book is written. A short essay for older readers/educators, titled 'Why were they hiding?', is included at the back of the book to help prepare teachers and others for the anticipated questions from children.

Transporting readers back in time in Australian history through this story will help young Australians to understand the reality of Aboriginal life under the various Protection Acts. The story will not instill fear because it is told with a sense of simple reality: this is how it was for the families and they did what needed to be done to protect their children from removal by government authorities. Rather than being a tool to teach young readers about the hideous aspects of Australian history, such as the injustices suffered by Aboriginal people, it can be seen as a book that shows how different the life experiences of most young Australians are today compared with those of young Aboriginal children of the past.

Fittingly, there is also a brief piece, 'About Daisy Bates', explaining the negative references to her throughout the book:

> Daisy Bates was famous for her writing and charitable work but not everyone liked her . . . In her popular book, *The Passing of the*

> *Aborigines*, she made it clear that she thought Aboriginal people were dying out, and she was also intolerant of 'half-caste' or mixed descent children . . . But . . . she used her own money as well as donations to provide food, clothing and basic medical care for her Anangu neighbours.[10]

The excellent book design by Louise Wellington and Brenda Thornley warrants particular mention. Text in language (also written phonetically) and English sitting side-by-side in the story, with explanations down the left-hand side of the page, assists in the reclamation of language, adding another dimension to an already culturally and socially significant product.

Language reclamation and maintenance are a priority for Aboriginal Australia. A book such as *Down the Hole*, which attempts to offer some level of both in its story, is more culturally valuable than many mono-lingual titles. Aboriginal words and phrases in children's books such as this one allow children from the language group to practise their own languages, while other children, Aboriginal and non-Aboriginal alike, can also learn the rich Yankunytjatjara, Kokatha and Matutjara languages. It is also a reminder to both educators and students that there were, and remain, distinctly different Aboriginal languages in Australia.

This work also has personal meaning for the illustrator, Kunyi June-Anne McInerney, herself taken at a young age, when she was known as Kunyi, and placed in the Oodnadatta children's mission where she was renamed 'Anne'. The illustrations are lifelike and at times sombre, but they are not depressing, thereby ensuring that young readers will not be put off or disturbed by the images. The children depicted look scared, of course, but no more scared than any child hiding from someone they know to be 'bad'. Today it would be called 'stranger danger'. The choice of subdued colours throughout makes a powerful statement.

Finally, Edna Williams says of writing this book that she saw it as a legacy for her grandchildren and great-grandchildren. For her it was a 'way of setting the record straight about what really happened to Aboriginal people with the "people-that-come-lately": that is, the rest of us'.[11] Likewise, co-author Eileen Wingfield says she was happy to make this book for her children, grandchildren and great-grandchildren. The generosity of spirit and wisdom wrapped up in the life experiences of these two Elders, and shared within the pages of this book, highlights the value Aboriginal people are placing in recording their own stories in the printed form for all Australians (and indeed international readers) to learn and grow from, either in an educational setting or simply reading alone at home or in the library.

Down the Hole is a book for all children and the many, many Australian adults who still need to grasp what happened in Australian history to stolen Aboriginal children in this country. In contrast, *Bush Games and Knucklebones* (2003) tells a story that is different from most books on the Stolen Generations. It looks at happy young children playing games in the Colebrook Children's Home at Oodnadatta in South Australia. Author Doris Kartinyeri spent fourteen years at Colebrook after being taken from her family soon after birth, and for her the book is a tribute to how the children at the home bonded to become a family for each other. The book is primarily about how they entertained themselves as children, playing games like 'knucklebones' (a game often called 'jacks' by young people in the 1970s). The rules for 'knucklebones' and 'kick the tin' are provided at the end of the book, so children today can enjoy the innocent and inexpensive games of the past as opposed to the violent video games of the present. A book that gets children 'doing' things is also a strategy for keeping young readers engaged in the story, with practical ways of making that story come alive for them.

This book shares the stories of 'secret gardens' and 'created playgrounds' where all that the children 'were interested in was the fun of building a pretend bus or truck'. The final lines of the book – 'We played these games daily – they made us happy and we shared with the other kids. Do you play imaginary games?'[12] – emphasises the shared experience of children being children, using their imagination and with no boundaries to friendship. It highlights what is possible with collaborative creativity. Accompanying the text are signature illustrations by Kunyi June-Anne McInerney (who also illustrated *Down the Hole*). The visual representation of the story in *Bush Games and Knucklebones* reinforces the truth of the sentiment behind Kartinyeri's words; the colours are alive and vibrant, in stark contrast to those used for the story in *Down the Hole.*

In terms of children's books attempting to discuss the many complex issues around Aboriginal identity, *Tell Me Why* (2004) is Sarah Jackson's story but it is also the story of so many other Aboriginal people dealing with society's preconceived ideas about Aboriginality and the use of skin colour to determine identity. At seven years of age, Sarah is simply a fair-skinned Aboriginal girl who goes to school, has dolls and plays chasey, just like other girls her age. White with freckles, though, one day she realises that her friends and family are different shades of colour and she starts asking questions like, 'Nana, how come I am Aboriginal like you, but you have brown skin and I have white skin?'.[13]

Sarah spends time with her Nana Mac and Grandma Doris and through asking questions and listening to her Elders she resolves the issue of marrying fair skin with Aboriginal identity. This was an issue for Sarah, one presumes, because many non-Indigenous Australians do not understand the historical constructions of Aboriginality. Aboriginality is based not on skin colour but on connection to country, kin, spirituality and life experience. Questions asked of Aboriginal people about their blood-quantum or grade of Aboriginality based on skin colour are highly offensive. They suggest that degrees of caste relate to degrees of identity, when for Aboriginal people the two are not linked at all.

Tell Me Why is an excellent tool for teachers to use in the classroom because it is an upbeat, positive story about Aboriginal identity in the twenty-first century. The questions that kids like Sarah ask are the same questions that are often asked of Aboriginal kids in the playground, and even of adults. They raise issues that Aboriginal people deal with on a daily basis, issues such as: 'How can you be an Aborigine if you've got fair skin, blonde hair, blue eyes, and live in the city?'. The list of questions I myself have been asked is endless. *Tell Me Why* gives an honest look at such questions through a child's eyes and the answers provided will help young people,

Aboriginal and non-Aboriginal, to understand how people like Sarah are Aboriginal and proud to be so.

The book is also successful in that, in a gentle and accessible way, history is provided about Aboriginal life prior to invasion, as well as the policy of protection and its consequences for those of the Stolen Generations and their families, including young Sarah. *Tell Me Why*, written with the assistance of Sarah's mother, Robyn Templeton, who also illustrated the text, will encourage students to research their own backgrounds and heritage, thereby contributing to a greater social conscience in terms of celebrating diversity in the Australian community.

Another identifying aspect of Aboriginal-authored books is that they often come with a moral. *Nana's Land* (2004), written and illustrated by Delphine Sarago-Kendrick, is an obvious example. This book is aimed at primary school-aged children, and the vibrantly illustrated story follows the journey of three Yidinji children, Warabul (the young hunter), his sister Kutabah and baby brother Bidu, to find their Nana Garna's country in Queensland's Atherton Tableland. The story combines adventure with the significance and responsibilities of coming-of-age, and highlights the role of storytelling in Aboriginal culture to pass on specific and important information about survival and history. The survival skills of Warabul and Kutabah are certainly tested when they find themselves separated from their extended family and must make their own way to their grandmother's homeland.

The moral to this story is not merely the importance of storytelling in Indigenous communities but also the role of story listening! It was Warabal and Kutabah listening intently to Nana Garna's stories that ensured they found her country later on, when they found themselves with no elders around to guide the way. Their safe arrival in the ranges meant that they had passed their first test and were well on their way to adulthood. The author, a descendant of the Yidinji and Jirrbal people of far north Queensland, dedicates the book to, among others, the stranger who gave her her first storybook, *Emanuel*, and reminds the reader of the significance of books for young people.

The Rain Flower (2005), written by Mary Duroux and illustrated by Yorta Yorta descendant Karen Briggs, is another moral story. A beautifully written and illustrated book, it tells the story of rain flowers and their role in maintaining a lush environment. While it is not a traditional Dreamtime story, the author (from the Yuin nation) says she has used the knowledge passed on to her by her elders. The story revolves around life near a dried-up waterhole, where the characters are night creatures (possum, wombat, bandicoot, curlew and owl) and day creatures (kangaroo, cockatoo, emu, echidna, pelican and goanna) who all struggle to find the special pink flowers with the red stalk that will make it rain. The creatures work together as a community to find the plant.

The story is delightfully complemented with both black-and-white and colour illustrations by Briggs who, as an artist, is inspired by the Barmah State Forest. *The Rain Flower*'s purpose, beyond encouraging young Indigenous kids to read, is to encourage young people to learn tolerance and how to work together. In addition, it is an environmental story and it highlights the negative effects that changes in the weather can have on the earth's creatures.

A language list and pronunciation guide at the back of the book make it possible to learn Dhurga language words for the night and day creatures. The book is pitched at six- to seven-year-olds and is designed as a first solo reader. Rhonda Black, publisher at Aboriginal Studies Press, notes that, while kids might need a bit of help with the language at the back, 'there's enough simplicity of language, repetition, simple morality etc. for the book to work just as well as a story that's read aloud to children, even though it's designed as a book for older children, with smaller black-and-white illustrations'.[14]

There is a further unique feature of Aboriginal-authored children's books that needs mention and that is the emergence of books written by very young Aboriginal kids. *The Cowboy Frog* (2003), targeted at three- to six-year-olds, is a story about a brave, blue-hat-wearing green frog near Noonkanbah Crossing who loved to fish for barramundi and was known as 'the Cowboy Frog'. Written and illustrated by Hylton Laurel when he was only nine years old, the story teaches kids that animals should only be hunted and killed for the purpose of eating and surviving, not for fun or sport. The illustrations are authentic and obviously drawn by a young person. A bilingual work combining English and the Walmajarii language (translations provided by Yangkana Madeleine Laurel), *The Cowboy Frog* is part of Magabala's Uupababa series, a collection of titles filled with bright illustrations for, and sometimes by, young children. The word *uupababa* is an Aboriginal word and is used extensively in the Broome area (where Magabala is located). It loosely translates as meaning 'little child' or 'baby'. *The Cowboy Frog* won an achievement award in the Multicultural Book Competition in 2004 and has set young Hylton up as a storyteller with promise. In the same year that *The Cowboy Frog* was published, seven-year-old Tamina Pitt released her book, *What Makes a Tree Smile*, co-authored with her mother, novelist and lawyer Terri Janke. As an art form, writing has fewer support mechanisms compared with the visual arts, dance and music, so Magabala Books is to be congratulated for opening their publishing doors to provide a platform for young voices. Books by young authors provide enormous support to the strategy of encouraging other young Indigenous kids to read, and hopefully write![14]

A final word on collaborative projects. Another title documenting language is *Creatures of the Rainforest* (2005), written by Anna Eglitis and Warren Brim. This work explores the Djabugay country of far north Queensland and is a collaboration between two friends from different cultures who wanted to use their art to celebrate friendship and reconciliation. Warren Brim is an Aboriginal man from the Djabugay clan and Anna Eglitis is a Fijian-born Australian of European descent. The pair met while Brim was a student of Eglitis's Aboriginal and Torres Strait Islander visual arts course at North Queensland TAFE.

Creatures of the Rainforest is a unique combination of art and factual information, as well as Aboriginal language and information from the Djabugay people of the area. The artists have studied a number of rainforest species, from ant to zamia palm, the mosquito to the quandong. It's also a unique and interesting way to teach young children the alphabet, as each artist presents his or her own personal and cultural perspective on each living organism. The book is aimed at upper primary school children to use as a starting point for further research into Australian native animals and plants and Aboriginal studies. However, younger children will also enjoy the artwork and the concepts when read with an adult.

The books that are being developed by Aboriginal individuals and communities working collaboratively speak for themselves in terms of the significant cultural product they provide to our children, our classrooms, our libraries, our home bookshelves, our international tourists. These books envelop the essence of Aboriginal storytelling and help to train children in the art of storylistening when they are read to. The works are clearly more than just words and pictures, because they speak of the histories, the cultures, the languages, the identities, the aspirations and the realities of the First Peoples of this land.

Writing for performance: Privilege, politics and goose bumps

Katherine Thomson

Back in 1981, when I was an actor at Theatre South in Wollongong, the New South Wales government gave substantial funding to the 'Women and Theatre Project'. The amount of funding was significant, $500 000 springs to mind, and the aim of the project was to redress the gender balance in the theatre by allowing women theatre practitioners to produce their own work in an extended festival. Having heard about Verbatim Theatre in Canada, and being curious about the apparent absence of working women in Wollongong, I applied for a tiny sum of money to research, write, produce and perform in a two-woman show with Faye Montgomery. I called the show *A Change in the Weather*, and, while a writer is always a different person once they have finished a work, it is fair to say that this show changed my life.

One of my most potent memories of the research was doing the rounds with a union official one morning when it was still dark. We visited a place where contract cleaners were working. I was introduced as someone who was writing a play. One of the women (a Greek migrant, if I remember correctly) took me by the arm and led me around a corner. 'Come here, darling,' she whispered, and then urgently told me how she was pressured by her supervisor to give bribes of expensive gifts, sometimes gold jewellery, in order to keep her job. 'You should put that in your play, darling,' she said. 'Can you put that in your play?'

The following Saturday afternoon I followed a notice I'd seen in a union office and attended one of the earliest meetings of women who had strange and unaccountable pains in their hands and wrists. The women worked in supermarkets stacking fridges and freezers or on the checkouts, or as typists or machinists, and they were given the information that they may well be suffering from a new phenomenon: tenosynovitis, carpel tunnel syndrome. When the person addressing the group asked people to raise their hands if they experienced pains in their hands and arms, I think I was the only person who didn't raise a bandaged hand.

Thus began my life as a writer, and the emergence of some of the characteristics of my work: themes of social justice and a set of community stakeholders who contribute to my (fictional) plays. Politics had always been a part of my life. As a child I read everything I could find on the civil rights movement in the United States and I had an uncle in Wollongong who would tell me the miners' side of the story during the tumultuous industrial period of the 1960s. We would sometimes visit him when they were 'out', and the gulf between his explanation for a current strike and that of the newspapers I read made a profound impression on me as a ten-year-old girl from Sydney.

It is fair to say that my plays are mostly concerned with the effect of social and economic change on 'ordinary people'. Over the years my plays have been about factory workers, barmaids in Fremantle, a whistleblower in a country town, ordinary people in Hong Kong before the handover, Aboriginal and non-Aboriginal pastoralists and graziers, the people of East Timor, a laundry woman in a hospital, and a former waterside worker and his family caught up in the Patrick's dispute. As for any writer of fiction, there is often a collection of characters swarming in my brain waiting for the right 'gig', so while my process may be to go out and interview people around a particular issue, these people are almost never directly represented on stage and may only partly influence the creation of the characters that eventuate. It is said that writers really only have one story, which they tell in different ways, and that writers often describe completing a work they had intended to be a departure from their usual style and themes only to read it and exclaim, 'Oh hell, it's me again'. I suppose my 'me again' is to do with love: the painstaking journeys we make to connect, in some small way, with another.

I hope the personal and political intertwine in my work, but my intention is almost always that the politics or the issue is a background against which the personal dramas are played out. The scope of the dramas I create is discussed in a book on Australian women writers, *The Dolls' Revolution*. There my characters are described as attempting 'minor revolutions within their own lives and those of the people around them. These pockets of resistance will be seen as moments of rebellion that effect minor, 'molecular' revolutions. These will be small shifts in attitude, changes in angles of vision or small, new starts'.[1]

To some degree I still measure the success of my work by the response of my 'community stakeholders', and it has been a privilege to enter so many different worlds in the course of my work. But primarily, as a dramatist, I write for actors and audience. My dramaturg, Paul Thompson, describes his position as a job-creation scheme for writers; I could say the same about myself and actors. I endeavour to write parts that a good actor will relish, in the hope that an actor will make it his or her own and develop the role beyond anything I had imagined. Dramatists write for that mysterious communion between actor and audience, writing something to be performed in real time and space in which people leave their homes to sit communally with a group of strangers in order to imagine, empathise, worry and laugh.

Some of the issues I have explored in my plays are microeconomic reform, whistleblowing and local government, redundancy in the workplace, the ballot for independence in East Timor, native title, and the Maritime Union of Australia (MUA)/Patrick's dispute. The ideas for these plays have come from many different sources. The idea for *Navigating*, for instance, a play set in a coastal Australian town engaged in a bidding war for a new private prison, sprang from a *Science Show* item about the Swedish ship the *Vasa*, launched in Stockholm Harbour in 1628. It was carrying sailors, shipwrights and many of their wives and children for the festive occasion. It was afloat for about ten minutes before sinking and drowning many of those on board. The ship appeared to have been top-heavy with extra cannon decks requested by the King.

Some years ago I began to think about the concept of whistleblowing, which was not then part of everyday parlance, and this led me to some initial meetings with a newly formed organisation then called 'Whistleblowers Anonymous'. I was put in touch with a few whistleblowers who had been many years battling out their cases in the courts, still suffering all manner of psychological stress from job loss, protracted legal battles and resultant financial problems, relationship breakdowns and loss of trust in a system they had believed in or individuals they had relied upon to help them. Thus began a rather tortuous path to what eventually resulted in a play about the value of dissidents in a town with dark secrets.

One woman I contacted began to send me information about her case in brown-paper envelopes, sometimes one a week. This process became vitally important to my understanding of how a small community could turn on a whistleblower, how toxic organisations can become, how destructive the rumour mill, and how detrimental to an individual's mental and physical health is the act of being a lone voice in an apparent wilderness. With this issue, as always, truth was indeed stranger than fiction. As an aside, so potent was this material, and so affecting, that I deliberately wrote a first draft before travelling to meet the woman. I wanted, at the time, to write a play about two sisters who had lived together for most of their adult lives, a story about what happened when one found love and wanted to leave the 'marriage'. Again, the exploration of these characters who had been somewhere in my subconscious for some years was as much a motivation as the issue at hand. And of course this was not her story. But I maintained the contact with her over the years of development. Her belief in the theatre as a potent force and one that could bring the elements of her painful story to light meant that she, of course, influenced my play in a fundamental way.

My responsibility, I believe, was to convey the essence of her experience, but I also had the writer's loyalty to my fictitious characters, these two sisters who became Bea and Isola in the play. I was equally bound by the issue and the art.

An issue no matter how 'worthy' does not always lend itself to drama, especially when the issue, rather than the story or characters, is a starting point. For instance, I was offered a number of commissions some time back to write a 'refugee' play. These offers came post-*Tampa*, and the incarceration of refugees in detention centres was something that many people, including myself, felt very passionate about. I was as active as I could be in my personal life lobbying against this cruel and illogical mandatory detention, but I could not see how to write a play about it, other than a montage-style verbatim work, a form I no longer wished to use. Also, I had written a play called *This Hospital My Country* for deckchair theatre a few years before – a play about displacement, with the central character being a Greek refugee from the Second World War. My point is that the decision to write a play is dependent on many different factors.

Perhaps the most crucial thing as a writer setting a narrative against a political event or an issue of social justice is to be prepared to be surprised, to be thrown off one's initial 'take' on an issue. One needs to be prepared to have one's initial sympathies overthrown and the drama will no doubt benefit from the writer's open mind. The characters, if realised fully, also work against didacticism, or should. A writer's challenge is to create characters who simultaneously serve the narrative being constructed while also having free will. This free will, this independence that a character develops, must take precedence over the political or social issues in a work. I was surprised at how well this need was understood by an official of the MUA when I asked if I could use their library and interview union members in preparation for *Harbour*. (For the younger reader it might help to understand that not so very long ago some branches of the maritime unions were known for their thuggish tactics.) He took me through to some other officials and the introduction went something like: 'This is Katherine. She's writing a play about the Patrick's dispute. She's writing a drama. As you all know – or should know – a drama is not polemical, it's not didactic. It'll have contradiction, paradox. She may not come down on our side.' He paused. I was taken aback but nodded approvingly. He gave a glimmer of a smile: 'But if she doesn't, we know where she lives.'

In Australia, if one is writing for any of the major theatres, it is very difficult to write about a current, topical issue. The lead-up for a play can be eighteen months. The decision to program a play in November of one year may have been made in April the previous year. There are other possibilities for one's work, of course – smaller companies, touring companies like Performing Lines, or production houses such as the Sydney Opera House/Malthouse Theatre.

The commitment by the Carr government in New South Wales in 1999 to build a brand-new 800-seat theatre was in itself a political act. We'd been through a federal election campaign in which some politicians fell over themselves to outdo each other to sneer at the 'elite arts', in the hope, presumably, that the millions of people in Australia who attended arts events would . . . What? Curl up and stay home to be relaxed and comfortable? Throw stones at writers and theatre directors and ABC drama producers to stop them going to work? It was hard to know and it was extremely depressing to endure this arts-bashing competition week in, week out. Elite sportspeople and elite businesspeople were not, thankfully, under similar attack so that was some comfort. Perhaps they were being saved up for the following election. However, by mid-2002 the theatre was on its way to completion in Sydney, preparing for an opening in January 2004, and the Sydney Theatre Company was going to manage it. The Sydney Theatre Company is on the harbour and the new theatre is across the road from the harbour. This was the largest new theatre that had been built in Sydney for many, many years.

At first when I was asked by Robyn Nevin, the artistic director of the company, to write a play to open the theatre I felt the responsibility was so enormous I ignored her emails and hoped they would go away. Robyn persisted. I said 'yes', tentatively, and hoped that an idea would come to me. Of some comfort was the plan to open the theatre with my play (about what?) in repertoire with a musical, using the same actors in both. A celebration of the actor as well as the building. The truth was I didn't have any ideas I thought worthy of the theatre or the company. This period, around 2002–2003, was a time of considerable turmoil in the world at large. There had been the September 11 attacks on New York and Washington, and we were all, whether we liked it or not, living in their aftermath. To an extent we were all fearful, not just of terrorism but also, perhaps even more so, of the US-led retaliation that was underway.

In the plays I had written over the years, many of the characters had been people struggling to cope with rapid social and political change and now I found I was one of them. I kept driving to the theatre company for meetings, floundering around in ideas, trying to define what I wanted to write about. As time went on, the company needed to know whether to get rid of me and find someone else, so the drives to the theatre were becoming increasingly tense and the meetings more frustratingly indecisive. The clock was ticking. The train was at the station ready to leave and I wasn't on it. Then finally, again going down to meet them to see 'where I was up to in my thinking', I decided to tell them that I couldn't do it and that they should find another writer.

And that day, as I drove along the road to the Sydney Theatre Company, I looked out of the car window and it suddenly hit me. About five hundred metres from the company are the shipping wharves: the cranes, the docks, the wharf labourers, the shipping containers. Right here, some five years earlier, this spot had been one of the sites of a raging national industrial dispute that was on the front pages of the newspapers for weeks. It had embroiled the unions, Patrick's Stevedoring and the Howard government in a bitter, hostile battle. It had been on television and in the courts.

Essentially, plans had been made to replace the Patrick's stevedoring workers with serving and former soldiers, trained in advance in Dubai. A corporate restructure meant that the workers were all dismissed – the notorious 'balaclava and dogs' night on Patrick's docks around the country – primarily for being members of a union. (Eventually, after two months in the courts and on picket lines, an agreement was reached between the

MUA and Patrick's, involving the dropping of all legal action against the company and it paying the expenses.) The dispute had galvanised the Australian public back in 1998. And it all seemed such a long time ago. It was before East Timor, before *Tampa*, before the Gulf War. This was a time when people in the military were starting to wonder if there was much future in the job, hence the attraction of training as stevedores in Dubai. The themes engaged me. I knew I had characters in my imagination who could find a place in this drama: an older man, a labourer, a bitter mother, a young working-class man studying the violin. These characters had been floating around in my head for some time and now they had a place.

Incidentally, I wasn't totally free in my casting of the play, and by that I don't mean the choice of actors but rather populating it with characters. The same actors would be in my play as would be in the musical, and the musical writers had already begun writing. So, unusually for a playwright, the ages and gender of the ten characters were pretty much prescribed to me. It seemed as good a starting point as any. The other certainty was that there would be a family, and the family's home, whether assisted housing or high-rise plush, would be within walking distance of the docks, and hence of the Sydney Theatre. Essentially, the political issue was an undeclared war, and so it made sense for the family in my play to be in a similar state. The discussions between Paul Thompson and myself, and Robyn Nevin and myself, were, in the early days, very much about values. And thus evolved Sandy, a man who perceives correctly that he has failed to pass on the core values of decency, fairness, responsibility and social justice to his children. He has abandoned his family, leaving a bitter, unforgiving wife, Val, who now vests her entire life in her youngest son who attends the Conservatorium of Music. Val is a very rigid character, and hopefully this is where her humour lies. In part, an area of interest for me with this play was the gap between true, creative flexibility and the much-touted contemporary workplace flexibility which basically means 'be available when we want you to work or we'll find someone else who will'.

John Raulston Saul says that embracing ethics means putting uncertainty at the centre of our lives and he writes of the dilemma of balancing our desire for certainty with our need for uncertainty. As much as I eventually wanted to celebrate Sandy's legacy to his family, I also wanted to critique union mythology, and Val and her children were particularly useful for that purpose, particularly the MUA organiser son, Matt, who was hissed at the previews by MUA members in the audience. Towards the end of the play, when the family is gathered around a funeral pyre upon which Sandy is about to be cremated, the same MUA members were outraged that the children were proud that they didn't know the words to the union anthem, 'Joe Hill'.

Originally I had toyed with the idea of creating a family divide between two brothers on either side of the dispute, and the violin-playing son was to be in the centre of the dispute and suffer when the corporate brother withdrew his financial support. I abandoned that idea after some weeks and settled instead on representing the stevedore's side of the argument through one of the SAS men who has gone to Dubai to train up as a 'scab' and also a younger man brought down from the country to 'scab' when the Dubai/SAS scheme went belly-up. I also wanted the SAS character for a very theatrical reason: I thought it would be a great opening to the play to have someone abseil into the performance space (as if in Dubai training on the docks). As things go, we swapped opening scenes the night before we opened, and, rather than opening with Dubai radio in Arabic and the abseil, we opened with Sandy on his way home taking a pee in Central Australia and reflecting on his journey ahead.

One of the reasons I'd had such trouble with coming up with an idea for the Sydney Theatre Company might have been that I was finishing off a play called *Wonderlands*, and starting to feel that I'd said just about everything I wanted to say about Australia, indeed about life. The theatre approached me, I think in 1999, to come up with a small list of the most significant events of the previous century, something I'd like to write about. I came up with about thirty different things I thought could be turned into a play. They weren't all thought through but they were broad, sweeping ideas. Ultimately I found none of them particularly inspiring after I'd sent them off. I sent them another note, in which I said I thought that the single most significant event was the day that a white pastoralist in Queensland, Camilla Cowley, had attended a meeting about a native title claim in Queensland and had walked from that meeting of mostly white pastoralists and graziers into the Native Title Office across the street and asked them to explain to her what this native title claim meant. This was the first time that a white Australian person had walked into that office and asked that simple question, and that meeting led to a well-publicised partnership between Camilla Cowley and Gunggari woman Ethel Munn. As is often the case after doing the research, I found that the story I thought I would tell, indeed the story between the two women that I had promised the theatre, began to crumble. I knew I was going to have to fictionalise it a lot more than I'd imagined.

For those not familiar with the Wik decision that was behind this highly charged, political focus, I quote Henry Reynolds's introduction to *Wonderlands*:

> It might not seem an ideal subject for an engaging play but a moment's thought will allow us to appreciate why Thomson set her play where she did. The Court, it might be remembered, decided that Pastoral Leases did not normally extinguish Aboriginal Native Title. This was a decision of almost revolutionary implications. Pastoral Leases covered vast areas of Outback Australia. They were the normal form of tenure for most pastoral families and had been so for two or three generations. Pastoralists thought of the land as theirs. Their families had often pioneered the land in question; had battled drought and flood and the banks; had buried grandparents and children and victims of accident. What is more, they often identified with their land.
>
> Before the Wik decision, no-one had challenged the tenure of leaseholders. They thought of themselves as proprietors with all the attendant status both in the country and in the Big Smoke. They were people of consequence. So Wik came like a thunderclap. Even when the case was under way all the advice given to pastoralists was that a lease by definition provided all the rights of a freehold title. Queensland leaseholders felt even more secure because their leases, unlike those in

> the other states, contained nothing about Aboriginal rights of access and use.
>
> The Wik decision, however, established that the Pastoral Lease was an inferior form of land tenure – little more than a licence to use the land for pastoral purposes. That alone was a great blow to status and prestige. What was even worse was the possibility that Aborigines with traditional association with the land in question could now claim traditional rights to use the land for traditional hunting and gathering and for ceremonial purposes.
>
> Clearly this outraged many pastoral families. Either many of the local Aboriginal families had been taken away to reserves and missions like Palm Island or Woorabinda or they lived on the outskirts of town in fringe camps and were at the very bottom of the hierarchy of status and esteem. What is more, the pastoralists of the 1990s had forgotten the brutal conflict that had so often accompanied the establishment of the pastoral industry and the critical role of Aboriginal labour once that conflict came to an end. The Aborigines had forgotten neither.
>
> For a few years after Wik there was a situation of tragic intensity. It passed largely unnoticed in urban Australia, at least in its specific, human detail.[2]

My challenge was to find a way through this abstract and ideological struggle to produce a compelling drama. Eventually the play became about Place and Belonging for both the Aboriginal and the non-Aboriginal characters. Continuity was an important concept and at one stage we (the directors Marion Potts, Wesley Enoch and myself) thought we would set the entire play on a single river; one location where multiple time frames could occur. That way we could go back and forward in history, reflecting the continuum in which Aboriginal people, in particular, regard their country and their stories.

A breakthrough for me occurred when I came across some books written in the 1930s by a woman called Alice Duncan-Kemp[3] which told of her time growing up as a young white girl on a property in Queensland. She described a complex but positive coexistence that had taken place on her parent's property between the Aboriginal people, the traditional owners, and her pastoralist father during the 1880s and 1890s. Alice had been initiated into an Aboriginal tribe when she was about six, and sections of the pastoral lands were off limits to grazing when Aboriginal ceremonies were taking place. This revelation and the discovery that many nineteenth-century Queensland pastoralists had endeavoured to raise awareness of the violence being perpetrated against Aboriginal people confirmed my decision to use a multiple time frame (two generations, the same land) and to work against audience expectations and show the white woman of 1931 in a positive light, thus playing with the idea of 'how it might have been'.

In the 1931 component of the story, Alice, a middle-aged white owner of the station, goes out riding for the day with Jim, an Aboriginal man. Jim has found a journal that another Aboriginal man had stolen from the house with some other things, and he gives it back to Alice in the course of the day. When Alice is given the journal, she reads her father's account of his earliest dealings with the Aborigines whose land he'd selected and leased. In this journal is documented the family tree of the Yirralong people and the ceremonies held on the sacred sites on the property. This information is crucial in the present-day native title claim. Subsequently Alice tells Jim – and the giving of the journal cements it – that she's going to leave the property to him. He is very sceptical about this proposal, knowing that all the other white graziers and pastoralists in the area would be firmly opposed to an Aboriginal man inheriting this property, but Alice is firm in her decision. She even writes a promissory note. However, she will fall from her horse and hit her head during the day and die before they can get back to town and make this promise legal. So Jim does not get the land. The land will go a man whose son will be Lon, now the third generation of this white family to inherit the pastoral lease.

Lon and his wife, Cathy, graze cattle. Their daughter is about to marry a young man called Tom from the neighbouring property, and Lon and Cathy hope that the couple will inherit both stations through the marriage alliance, in order to keep this enlarged property, now called 'Ambertrue', in the family. When the Yirralong people lodge a native title claim, Lon is outraged that his plans are threatened. This claim produces a level of hysteria in the white pastoralists of whom Lon is the chief representative. Also, of course, because this would have been terribly boring and one-sided as a tale, I seeded in conflict between the Indigenous people themselves in the native title claim. There was, in fact, a conflict between two of the Aboriginal groups in the area in which I had done my initial research. The signatory to the Native Title, Edie, is herself conflicted, in part because she has to please so many parties (including the deceased Elders) but also because she herself is a grazier, essentially with a foot in both camps. She doubts her ability to follow through.

The last scenes of the play are of reconciliation, and belong to the women. Cathy's daughter has run away from home when the play begins, and Cathy has spent much of the play trying to track her down. (She appears to have suffered some sort of mental illness, and the longed-for marriage between her and the property owner next door will never take place.) In the last scenes of the play – after Lon and Tom have committed the terrible crime of trying to blow up ancient rock art at a significant site in order to destroy evidence of Aboriginal presence on their land – Cathy hands over the family journal to Edie; this set of records may help Edie prove connection to the land as part of the native title claim.

Wonderlands was the first time I had written specific Aboriginal characters for stage or film. (Of course, over the years I've written roles that Aboriginal actors have played, but I mean roles that were *about* being Indigenous Australians, roles that could not be played by non-Indigenous actors.) This kind of writing, and the relationship I had developed with Ethel Munn and her son Bob, created certain obligations which I hope I was able to fulfil. Drafts were sent to Mrs Munn to read prior to rehearsal. I kept her informed of my progress over the long development period, heeding her warning not to be a 'whitefella swinging on black coat-tails'. I endeavoured to keep abreast of the progress of the Gunggari native title claim. On one memorable day I had the privilege of being in a Sydney courtroom that was linked by video to a Brisbane courtroom while one stage of the Gunggari claim was being heard.

It is sometimes said that there is an inclination these days for our major producers, in theatre and public broadcast television, to shy away from work that will attract negative political attention and might affect their government funding or corporate sponsorship. While not denying that other writers may have experienced such stonewalling or interference, it has not been my own experience. In the examples above, *Harbour* and *Wonderlands*, there would have been a myriad of reasons for the companies to steer me towards other subject matter. *Wonderlands* was written for Hothouse Theatre in Albury–Wodonga. Would a regional audience, an audience that would have been much more directly affected by the issue of native title, want to see a play about the same? The company did not flinch. They supported the idea from day one, despite the fact that it was an enormous financial commitment (research, workshopping) as well as a risk to make a piece of theatre around such controversial material. The play was, thankfully, a success in Albury–Wodonga, Wagga Wagga and then at the Griffin Theatre in Sydney. Sadly, plans were dropped to do a tour around regional Australia the following year due to a lack of enthusiasm from the management of theatre complexes in other parts of regional Australia.

Robyn Nevin commissioned *Harbour* with great conviction and support. But due to the sensitivity of the material, it was very likely that neither the prime minister nor any other federal minister would attend the prestigious and important opening day of the new Sydney Theatre, and indeed this is what happened. The matter of a corporate sponsor was another issue (readers might be shocked to know that only 7.5 per cent of funding for the Sydney Theatre Company is from government) because the major sponsor for the *Republic of Myopia* musical (in repertoire with *Harbour*) was P&O, the stevedoring company. P&O had not been directly involved in the dispute but would clearly not be an appropriate sponsor. A search for an alternative sponsor was undertaken and happily Phillips Fox stepped up to the crease as Presenting Sponsor for *Harbour.*

When I was approached to co-write the mini-series *Answered by Fire*, I knew that over the years a number of my colleagues had tried to put the East Timor story on the screen but their scripts were still languishing unproduced. By 2002, however, the time was apparently right to dramatise the 1998 East Timor push for independence. The ballot for independence was still fresh and the Howard government's motivation for supporting it was under increased scrutiny, in part because of discussion about a pro-Jakarta lobby in the Department of Foreign Affairs and Trade and also because of the Timor Gap (oil and gas) Treaty then under negotiation.

This was my second project 'about' East Timor. A few years earlier I had co-written a play for deckchair theatre in Fremantle, *Mavis Goes to Timor,* a highly successful work which had done a couple of national tours. Producers Simpson Le Mesurier, for whom I'd written *Snowy* and *Halifax f.p*, knew about *Mavis* and invited me to write a TV mini-series with Canadian writer-producer Barbara Samuels. The initiative for the show came from Barbara. Helped by the financial attraction of a co-production between CBC Canada and ABC TV we began our research in East Timor, to find a way to tell the drama of the newest country on the planet and its ballot for independence from Indonesia in 1999.

Barbara, like most Canadians, knew very little about East Timor, other than she'd been inspired by two Canadian Mounties who had served as UN Civpol during the violent lead-up to the ballot. Civpol were the unarmed Civilian Police brought in before the ballot to support the Indonesian Police who had been tasked with providing security to the East Timorese against the increasingly violent gangs of militia. We know now that these militia were supported by the Indonesian military (TNI) in order to undermine the ballot, and then to raze East Timor to the ground in a 'scorched earth' policy, in the event of a vote for independence from Indonesia. The impossible task of standing up to the TNI and the police's dawning realisation of its orchestrated plan became the core of our drama. (The police were behind the eight ball, of course. The East Timorese knew exactly what was going on, but cops being cops need tangible evidence. It was good dramatic material.)

There were many ways to tell this story. Other teams may have chosen to tell it via the decision-makers: the high drama of week-long meetings of the Security Council in New York, for example, or perhaps a drama around the Defence Intelligence Organisation. But Barbara and I both felt that we could cover politics *and* deliver a satisfying emotional story if we entered the East Timor drama via a lead Australian Federal Police officer, a Canadian Mountie and a young East Timorese student.

We knew that East Timorese characters had to be central, as it was their story. We took a gamble that there were actors who would be able to play major roles, and thanks to sensitive casting, committed producers and a director (Jessica Hobbs) who knew how to help less experienced actors find their feet, the finished product had superb performances all round: Canadian, Australian and East Timorese.

That the East Timorese were on-screen telling their story in their own language could be seen as a political act in itself. There were small battles to be won – the use of subtitling is not popular in Canadian prime-time. Indeed, the Canadian network had had a change of guard since the initial commissioning and was going cold on the show even while we were writing later drafts. For a time it looked as if we wouldn't get up. The Canadian national broadcaster had had enough of 'serious political' drama, it seemed, and had their sights set on comedy and light entertainment. Eventually it was poorly promoted on CBC Canada and disappeared into a poor timeslot. But, small comfort, it was well reviewed. The collective nature of television allows me to include an extract of a review from Toronto's *Globe and Mail*: 'Unsettling in its unnerving devotion to telling all aspects of the story, wrenchingly realistic and emotionally complex, *Answered by Fire* is never easy to watch, yet it's impossible to look away. It is a brilliant piece of drama. Simply some of the best television ever.'[4]

The ABC did not flinch in its support for *Answered by Fire*. Robyn Kershaw commissioned the drama under Sandra Levy and both were extremely enthusiastic. Scott Meek was head of Drama after Robyn and got us over the line. Inevitably, no matter how personal a story one creates, a drama about East Timor will be critical of the United Nations, the Australian federal government, the Suharto government in Indonesia and the Indonesian military. In the years our show was in development, the ABC appeared to be under siege from some conservatives, accusations of left-wing bias were flying thick and fast, and overall the ABC budget was diminishing. Drama hours were way down. By the time our show was made it wasn't just part of a drama slate; it was almost the *entire* slate.

East Timor has been a hot issue in Australia since the Indonesian invasion of 1975 and a particularly sharp thorn in the side of Australia's relationship with Indonesia since the ballot of 1999. Some time before our show was shown on the ABC, a document was released by a member of the military which spoke of a 'Jakarta lobby' inside Defence Intelligence, Australian officials who are agents of the Indonesian state apparatus. It claimed that Australians who challenge the orthodoxy of this lobby are marginalised and that many inside military intelligence were concerned. This was interesting in light of the following scene from the second half of *Answered by Fire*, once the Australian Federal Police are back in Australia.

EXT. SAME – LATER

Liz settling on the bench. Hands them the takeaway coffees.

Liz: OK.

Ron (deferring to Mark): I'm just here as moral support.

Mark: I've been offering myself as an expert witness for the two months since we got back . . . I've got the documentation, the backup, whatever they need. No one wants to know. (with difficulty) Maybe it's not news but . . . I'll talk to you if you . . . if you'd definitely do something with it.

Liz: You're not the only one.

I've got a whistleblower. In military intelligence.

Mark: What's he saying?

She hesitates. He looks at her, *tell me.*

Liz: Look, I'm right in the middle of the story, and I really should be keeping my mouth shut.

A difficult moment as she and Mark stare at one another. Finally:

Liz (cont'd): He saw stuff coming in on Timor all year. He knew it was going to explode. Defence intelligence was listening to every phone call the Indonesian military made. They heard all the planning, heard them give the militia their orders . . . who they were supposed to kill, when . . . sometimes *how.*

Mark: While we were risking our arses advising them on 'security'.

Liz: He claims there's a pro-Jakarta group inside defence intelligence that overrides dissenting opinion 'cause the government doesn't want to hear it.

She watches as Mark tries to absorb this.

Liz (cont'd): To maintain our 'special relationship' with Indonesia.

Mark: So we were up there, unarmed, even while they're getting all this intelligence.

She shrugs. That's it.

Ron: They just took a punt none of us'd be killed.

(pause) What a bunch of fucking mugs we were.

Just before we aired, Australia and Indonesia announced that they were looking forward to a new, more positive phase in diplomatic relations. I wondered if our four-hour drama might set this back a few years (the TV series *Embassy* hadn't done a lot for Malaysia/Australia relations some years previously), but it seems to have gone unremarked in diplomatic circles.

Television production, particularly high-end drama, has been in decline in Australia for some years. When *Answered by Fire* was aired, it was embraced as a TV drama series that was rare in its relevancy, in its tackling of a complex issue. As I mentioned earlier, the ABC drama budget has been whittled away until it has become a disgrace. We should be demanding more challenging, quality drama from all our networks, including the commercial ones. As for the latter, we pay for it, after all, whenever we buy anything that's been advertised on TV. We deserve to be nourished.

In Jane Wagner's one-woman play for Lily Tomlin, *Search for Signs of Intelligent Life in the Universe*,[5] one of the many characters Tomlin plays is a bag lady, Trudy, guiding some inquisitive visitors from outer space around New York. In an early scene they ask her what goose bumps are: do they come from the heart? Soul? Brain? Or do they come from geese? Trudy has trouble answering this question. So she moves on to an explanation of the difference between a can of Campbell's soup and Warhol's painting of a can of soup. No matter how many times she says 'This is soup. This is Art. Soup. Art. Soup. Art', she cannot get through to them. And they are no closer to understanding goose bumps. So she takes the Martians to the theatre. In the final scene, under a night sky, the bag lady relays to her own audience what happened:

> Did I tell you what happened at the play? We were at the back of the theatre, standing there in the dark; all of a sudden I feel one of 'em tug my sleeve, whispers, 'Trudy, look'. I said, 'Yeah, goose bumps. You definitely got goose bumps. You really like the play that much?' They said it wasn't the play gave them goose bumps. It was the audience. I forgot to tell 'em to watch the play; they'd been watching the audience.

If ever there was a need, in my lifetime anyway; for citizens to be able to expand their imaginations, their empathy to the 'other', to sit as an audience and worry collectively, to give themselves over to mystery and to possibility, the time is now. Despite the often political/personal blend of my own work, in terms of *changing* our society I long ago came to the conclusion that, to paraphrase the poet J. M. Flecker, drama might not change people's souls, but at the very least it will make them glad they have one. It's enough to keep me going.

Travelling towards ourselves: Rights and recognition in Clara Law's *Letters to Ali*

Bernadette Brennan

Clara Law acknowledges that, as a filmmaker, her 'craft' is more powerful than her voice.[1] In *Letters to Ali* (2004) she uses that craft skillfully to take her viewers on a journey, both physical and moral, towards an understanding of the plight of asylum-seekers in Australia today. *Letters to Ali* grew out of Law's discovery that an Anglo-Australian family had established – through letters, phone calls and one visit – a powerful relationship with a fifteen-year-old Afghan boy detained in the Port Hedland detention centre after being smuggled out of Afghanistan to the safety of Australia by his father in 2001. When this family, the Kerbis, set out on their second 8000 kilometre trek through the centre of Australia to visit 'Ali',[2] Law and Eddie Fong, equipped with a DV camcorder, went along. Law was unsure about how the film would take shape but she knew two things: that the issue of children in detention needed urgent attention; and that the film she would make would be 'more like a documentary [or] an essay film', because the story of an incarcerated, unaccompanied minor needed no dramatisation.

Letters to Ali remains true to Grierson's principles of documentary film in that it is 'a creative treatment of actuality'[3] constructed with a clear social purpose in mind. It is a film designed to educate Australians about the injustice currently being dealt to asylum-seekers. It operates on a visual and visceral level to ensure that we – the Australian audience – come to really see what a democratic 'fair go for all' Australia means when one attempts, without an entry visa, to seek shelter within our borders.

Law contacted Dr Trish Kerbi after reading, and being deeply moved by, an article written by her, 'Walking in their shoes', published in the Melbourne *Age* in September 2002. In that piece Kerbi wrote:

> The reason I began writing to Ali was that I had a strong feeling our media reports are often biased, if not completely inaccurate . . . It seems we Australians have been allowed to see the problem of boat people through a tiny keyhole and that the government determines our viewing angle. I decided to write because I wanted to change the view and try to see the big picture (*Saturday Extra*, p. 6).

Letters to Ali is Law's response to that predetermined viewing angle. She is interested in showing us a less sanitised, broader view of detention and its implications than we have previously been offered. Kerbi's 'tiny keyhole' analogy is correct in the way it signifies that the federal government has tried to restrict our view of asylum-seekers, but much of that obstruction has been achieved by offering the public a large, generalised picture where asylum-seekers have become known as an amorphous group rather than as individuals. Law counteracts that strategy by focusing her interest on the plight of a particular boy, Ali. Of course, no cameras or recording equipment are allowed inside detention centres, so the temporal world of the film focuses largely on the family's journey. Law disrupts that physical journey repeatedly with interviews and written commentary that serve to reinforce the voice and message of the film. Having voluntarily placed ourselves into the captivity of the cinema for 105 minutes, we are taken on a number of journeys, all of which function to take us outside the comfortable parameters of our (predominantly urban) lives where the reality of distant detention centres can easily pass unnoticed.

The six-minute opening sequence that precedes the film's title immediately frames Law as a migrant filmmaker. We read: 'I am a filmmaker. I used to live on a small island.' We hear the muted sounds of Hong Kong Harbour as the camera's eye sweeps broadly over the working ferries to a view from the narrow rectangular windows of a Hong Kong skyscraper, high above the city traffic, shielded from, but conscious of, the sirens below. The next caption tells us: 'Eddie and I settled down in Australia in 1995.' The background colour is pale blue, the music is calm and beautiful – this has been a peaceful relocation, a move from a crowded, noisy metropolis to a silent and seemingly empty landscape.

The wide Australian suburban streetscapes are recognisable from Law's *Floating Life* (1996) but in this film they teem with natural life and beauty. There is an explosion of colour, the busyness of pollinating bees, the birth and nurturing of baby birds. Law has 'never lived so close to the earth'. The camera is more grounded and the views are horizontal rather than vertical. There is (an unnerving) silence and too much space. This is the beginning of a recurring theme: Australia is a vast and under-populated country. For three minutes Australian viewers, perhaps more atuned to viewing the suburbs as sites of satire – Moonee Ponds and Fountain Gate – discover how beautiful and peaceful suburbs can be. Perhaps we have learnt to take them and the lifestyle they afford for granted. Through the lens of this migrant filmmaker we see them anew. Later we will come to understand how they have been positioned in stark contrast to the isolated and isolating Baxter and Port Hedland detention centres.

There are multiple layers of migration stories at work in the film. From the outset links are made between Ali's incarceration and the reception afforded to Rob Silberstein (Trish Kerbi's husband) when he arrived in Australia as a child of two with his parents, fleeing the horrors of postwar Europe. In the 1940s the Silbersteins were placed in a migrant camp which functioned not as a deterrent to others but as a site of education and assistance. Rob's family history operates as a challenge to, and a warning against, the continuance of mandatory detention for refugees, particularly young refugees. Comparisons between Australia's current policies of detention and the atrocities perpetrated under the Nazis are made repeatedly. In her first interview Trish outlines how she and Rob were affected by their trip to Dachau concentration camp and how she found it incomprehensible that those living in the vicinity of the camp remained ignorant of what was going on. She wonders why no one tried to 'stop or interfere with what Hitler was doing'. Trish is surprised to find on her return home that there are camps in Australia. She discovers how difficult it is to obtain information about these camps. She knows that she is morally compelled to 'take the time to become acquainted with what was happening'. *Letters to Ali* exhorts its audience to do likewise. In her article Trish notes the proximity of the town of Port Hedland, population 15 000, to the detention centre. The film, however, emphasises how remote these places are for most Australians and the ease with which out of sight can mean out of mind. Both Trish and Law decide to 'find out more' about the human impact of Australia's detention policies. The film shares that knowledge with its audience.

Letters to Ali is a film deeply concerned with correspondence. The initial relationship between Trish's family and Ali was one of letter writing. Trish then corresponded with the general public through her article in the *Age*. Clara in turn corresponded with Trish and worked with her family to make the film. Once Law and Fong began telling their friends and colleagues about the project, a huge collaborative effort got under way: 'People threw in their support,' we read, 'editing, mixing, video mastering, an editor, composer, sound designer, lawyer . . .'. The film can be viewed as Law's correspondence with us, not only through her use of captions, which can be read as mini-postcards, but also in the sense that it demands a response: an acknowledged responsibility towards an 'other'.

The title of Trish's article, and her comment that she 'wanted to try to walk for a short while in their [refugees'] shoes before I passed judgment on them', opens up the possibility of empathic identification. Of course such identification is not possible when we have not suffered the trauma of war, torture, dislocation and indefinite incarceration. Law understands this predicament. She sets out to ensure that we come to a greater understanding of the plight of asylum-seekers. She demonstrates how it is possible for 'ordinary' Australians to accept some responsibility for what is happening and, in their response, to change things for the better. Law is never didactic. She understands how images operate as a mode of knowing. She also knows that the viewers' capacity for receiving images is determined by their capacity to interpret them. That is why she takes us on a journey using images, mood and music to inform our aesthetic emotions.

Paul Grabowsky's musical score is one of the most powerful and political features of this film. The haunting piano offers moments of genuine peace and beauty that heighten the horror of the razor-wire imagery and the introduction of clashing symbols that evoke the slamming shut of steel doors. Much of the score is in a minor key. There are crescendos and intensifications of chords which darken our mood and fill us with apprehension. A clear example of this intensification occurs as the family approach an isolated Aboriginal settlement. We cut from inside the four-wheel drive where the Kerbi children are singing raucous rounds of a silly song to the ominous music and a slow panning shot of an upturned rusted car body. The music continues while Trish's voice-over reads from her article about the Taliban brutality that forced Ali's father to have his son smuggled to safety. At this moment the piano is joined by the cello, and a little later the double bass, as the family pass through the desolate township. Time seems to slow. The four-wheel drive decelerates, the music slows. Long shots filmed through the windscreen pick out more abandoned cars, mangey dogs and the one sturdy building in town, an incongruous (and for the climate inappropriate) A-frame orange-brick Baptist church. Its perimeter fence is intact. Sounds merge so that the crescendo of sorrowful music dialogues with the crying crows. Dust, filmed in front of a blazing setting sun, shrouds the scene. As the few Aboriginal inhabitants, standing silent by the roadside, are captured unfocused in the grainy, shaky film, we read: 'They die younger than other Australians, by 20 years.' At this moment we understand that Ali is not the only person who has come to this land uninvited. Law makes no direct statements, but the tone of the images, the fading light and the music ensure that we understand what she is saying.

Much of the film is taken up with the 8000 kilometre journey from rural Victoria to Port Hedland and as such *Letters to Ali* can be read as another Australian road movie. The journey through the centre is like so many journeys to the centre in Australian film – *Wake in Fright, The Last Days of Chez Nous, Priscilla: Queen of the Desert, The Proposition, Wolf Creek* – a journey into knowledge. For Law it is also, to some extent, a celebration of the magnificent Australian outback. Like the suburban gardens of the opening scenes, the outback is shown to us in all its majesty. There is no mistaking, however, that the terrain Law shows us, and through which we must journey, is a moral one as much as a physical one. The frequency of wide shots of unpopulated vistas emphasises the contrast with Hong Kong and wordlessly asks why Australia needs to lock up asylum-seekers fleeing crowded, war-torn countries. Joyous scenes of the Kerbi children skylarking on outback roads, spinning freely under brilliant blue skies, being comfortable enough in their bodies to demonstrate their various piercings, speak to the inability of a boy of the same age to do such things or to know such freedom. This extraordinary world of contrast and wonder is 'the world outside the walls'. It is not something Ali can see or be a part of. Ali's life is 'shown' to us through words set against ominous-looking treetops, glowering skies and tumultuous seas. His landscape is very different from Law's: razor wire, security cameras, steel gates. The family does not reach Port Hedland until fifty-five minutes into the film. Law makes her viewers sit through that time for a number of reasons: first, it builds a sense of dramatic expectation; second, it emphasis how far away these detention centres are from the major cities; third, it makes us wait, just like Ali has to wait, for any resolution. Unlike Ali, we are reassured at various intervals, through the use of maps and captions, that we are progressing towards a goal.

Another powerful strategy Law employs is the use of silence. If we were to close our eyes at the beginning of the film we would hear nothing but the occasional piece of music for six minutes. We would not know about Law's history or how she came to find out about Trish and Ali. We would not know how she met Trish or that she had decided to make the journey to Port Hedland. We would hear, at a little after six minutes, Erin Kerbi's rippling laughter, followed by ominous music. One of the messages of this film is that it is very easy to close our eyes, to not see the inhumane treatment being meted out to those who come to Australia seeking asylum. As

David Marr has noted: 'Australians believe what's done to deter asylum-seekers . . . has no impact on themselves. They imagine they are somehow quarantined from their own brutality.'[4] *Letters to Ali* refuses to allow us that distanced perspective. In place of dialogue or voice-overs, Law uses captions designed by Sarah Lucy. The captions are presented in two or three striped bands. Visually they suggest rigidity or containment. When they tell of Ali sewing his lips together, they can be read as his scars. The writing in this and other brutal sections changes from green to red. By forcing the audience to read the captions, Law ensures that we become active participants in her unfolding narrative. We are drawn into the process of her discovery of, and distress over, the inhumane treatment of asylum-seekers.

At times the captions appear alone on the screen, at other times they are coupled with images. To marry an image with text is always, as Roland Barthes has argued, to add to or narrow the meaning already present.[5] Most often Law's captions operate to demonstrate the enormous gulf between what we might read and what we might feel, that is, the gulf between our intellectual appreciation of 'facts' and the actual situation. Ten minutes into the film we witness full-screen amateur footage of the beginning of the 2002 Easter riots outside the Woomera detention centre. The diegetic noises (real-life sounds, as opposed to fabricated sounds such as voice-overs and soundtracks) are a cacophony of those behind the wire calling for assistance, those outside chanting 'freedom' and 'free the refugees', and the metallic sound of fences being shaken. The hand-held camera is extremely unsteady. A sense of impending chaos pervades. It is then we are presented with our first caption, alone on the screen: 'SOME FACTS ABOUT ASYLUM SEEKERS'. But before we find out these 'facts', we are again offered a full-screen image of dozens of asylum-seekers clutching the wire fence and looking into the camera. The sound quality is poor but we hear one tearful woman say she has been in detention for nineteen months. And then the image is brought into an increasingly sharp focus. It shrinks to a small square surrounded by blackness. Superimposed on the images – which are mostly of young children – we read: 'I want my father, I want visa.' For two further minutes Law offers us simultaneously captions informing us that 'Australia is one of the signatories to the United Nations Refugee Convention 1951' and that our government has instituted this policy of detention as a means of border protection and deterrence, and images of the contorted, miserable faces of incarcerated people clutching at fences. At this point the only sound is Grabowsky's piano score, but for a few minutes, thanks to the actual footage, we have been transported vicariously to this site; we have heard the noise and experienced a taste of the atmosphere. We cannot help but be moved by the emotive images and distressing noise. We are forced to question the justice of the government's policy by understanding, through felt experience, the gap between what we read and what we see and feel.

Law exploits this strategy further when she interviews Adam Myonvell, a musician who was present at the riots and was later charged with harbouring escapees. A documentary film, to achieve its social function, requires a certain level of authenticity. Interviews are a particularly powerful form of providing credibility, not only because we hear eyewitness accounts but also because we hear inflexions in the voice and see the interviewees' body language, their facial expression, how they say what they say. Law defers offering us this interview until she feels (correctly) that we are ready to hear and appreciate what is being communicated to us. Myonvell is interviewed in front of his drum kit in an orderly, quiet environment. He is clean-shaven, glowing with health. He is young and good-looking. His testimony of the harrowing events of that day is spliced with actual footage of the escape. As he struggles to find the words to describe the pointed fence spike, as he describes the blood caused by slashes from razor wire, as he becomes visibly moved by his memories, we see the bright red blood flowing and we hear the desperate yelling and screaming of people on both sides of the wire. The voices of those incarcerated are all the more powerful because of their previous silence to us. The camera angle of the actual footage zooms in on, and dips below, the belly of the charging police horses. The uncertainty and chaos that results from the collapsed fence and the escaped refugees is palpable. The noise is terrifying. Myonvell begins to stumble on his words as he recounts the mayhem and the confusion. In relief we laugh with him when he recounts how he was mistaken for an escapee – a humorous aside which also questions implicitly the arbitrary divide between the 'us' and 'them'.[6]

Adam Myonvell is a very likeable character. His question, 'When is there a law that is wrong?', is a crucial question this film encourages us to ask. Again there is a link with Nazi Germany. A version of that question was asked by a number of German thinkers, particularly Gustav Radbruch, once a firm defender of the 'positivist' doctrine. A 'positivist' is defined as someone who insists 'that once the rule is laid down or determined, it does not cease to be law because it may be shown to be in conflict with morality'.[7] Radbruch, having experienced the Nazi regime, decided that the 'positivist' doctrine was morally wrong and called on his contemporaries to renounce it. H. L. A. Hart explains the implications of what follows if the doctrine of the separation of laws and morals is discarded: 'if laws reach a certain degree of iniquity then there would be a plain moral obligation to resist them and to withhold obedience'.[8] Myonvell puts it more simply: 'People decided that people should help people.' Most Australians, removed from the reality of detention, do not think about such issues. Many would say any resemblance to what is happening legally to asylum-seekers here is a far remove from what occurred in Nazi Germany. It is important, therefore, that we remember the High Court ruling on Ahmed Al-Kateb, a stateless man who arrived in Australia by boat in December 2000. The media showed very little interest in this ruling and yet the High Court, by a majority of four to three, ruled that it was permissible to keep Mr Al-Kateb, a person innocent of any wrong-doing, in detention for the rest of his life as a practical means of preventing 'people from "entering or remaining in the Australian community"'.[9] Indeed, as Justice Ken Hayne argued, it was only possible to incarcerate Mr Al-Kateb indefinitely because he was innocent of any crime. His detention could not, therefore, be classed as punishment. As Marr states: 'On 6 August 2004, when the court handed down its verdict, Australia discovered it was a rare country in the free world where a government minister has the power, all on her own, to imprison innocent people, perhaps forever.'[10]

There are further interviews which contribute to the authenticity and authority of this documentary. Interviews with Trish Kerbi establish the groundwork of how her relationship with Ali eventuated and how it grew to be mutually enriching for Ali and all her family. Law's seemingly rough editing style also lends an air of authenticity. Initially we wonder why a phone call from Trish's son, Rian, asking her to bring home marshmallows is allowed to intrude on the important interview early in the film. The answer is because it demonstrates how easy it is for Australian teenagers to communicate with their mothers, to make requests and to expect reasonably to have them met. The banality of Rian's request makes this point of communication all the more powerful.

Law's interviews with Trish's and Rob's four children are crucial for establishing the film's credibility. Their testimony about the inside of the detention centres is honest and unscripted. We have been told about the security equipment, the guards, the fences and the compounds of the centres, but these facts become more real when six-year-old Erin talks of feeling sick when she went through the gates, of being scared, of not wanting to stay. Hannah's most vivid memories of her first visit are of barbed wire, metal, gates and guards. She admits that she did not want to go in because 'it was so horrible'. She expected Ali to have 'darker skin'. Rian was 'shy about talking to a refugee'. He didn't know how to treat him, but after fifteen minutes of talking 'he was like a normal friend – it was really cool'. These interviews are of central importance in a film designed to convey the message that it is 'ordinary' Australians, people 'just like us', that can make a constructive difference to asylum-seekers and the policies that govern them.

Law carefully withholds certain interviews for maximum effect. Ian McPhee, with his title of Minister for Immigration and Ethnic Affairs 1979–1982, is introduced after thirty minutes. He follows on from the script informing us that opinion polls in 2001 showed that a majority of Australians had negative feelings about refugees and that the Minister at the time had said he would not release people who could possibly be 'murderers and terrorists'. McPhee's words are a response to this politics of fear. From his airy, rural home he outlines the arrival of boat people from

Vietnam, Cambodia and Laos in the 1970s. He speaks of our obligation to take these refugees fleeing a war in which Australian troops supported American forces. Iraq and Afghanistan are never mentioned but hang thickly in the air, the point is made.[11] The difference, we are told, between then and now is to do with 'statesmanship'. It is at this point we remember one of Law's earliest captions about arriving in Australia and being able to cast her vote for a new government for the first time. Her vote 'did not help the losing party win'. Again the implications are left for the viewer to interpret: How legitimate are these laws? Is our system of representative democracy adequate? Are the wishes of the majority being enacted? If not, are there ways to make Australian democracy more participatory? How can citizens make a difference to the laws being enacted on their behalf?

The interview with former prime minister Malcolm Fraser is withheld until the final stages of the film. With his towering frame and authoritative voice, Fraser, filmed in close-up in his home library, fills the screen and exudes a certain *gravitas*. He is given more time than any of the other interviewees and he states his message clearly: that the federal government has manipulated the Australian people through a politics of fear; that difference is not something we should be afraid of; that asylum-seekers pose no threat to Australia's borders; and that children should not be imprisoned without just cause. Fraser uses the evils of Nazi Germany as a point of comparison with the manufactured fear of refugees currently occurring in Australia. This fear left unchecked, he cautions, has the potential to spread and destroy the moral fabric of our society. He exhorts our political leaders to learn from past atrocities and 'fight discrimination, racism, hatred, religious bigotry with all the force and all the persuasion they can use'. We need to 'strive', he says, 'to recognise what justice really means'.

Law could be criticised for omitting any interviews that offered a contrary view to the voice of the film which decries the detention of refugees. *Letters to Ali*, however, sets out to fill the void of information created by a deliberate policy of government censorship. Natascha Klocker and Kevin Dunn have demonstrated convincingly that the federal government's regulations restricting media access to asylum-seekers meant that, at least during the period of their study, August 2001 to January 2002, media outlets became reliant on government press releases as their primary source of information about asylum-seekers. The unrelenting negativity and the perjorative language used by the government to describe asylum-seekers – the most common terms being 'illegal', 'illegitimate' and 'threatening'[12] – shaped the negative impression readers developed about the 'problem' of asylum-seekers. They note: 'By presenting asylum-seekers as not entitled to protection and by differentiating them strongly from genuine refugees, government constructions worked to justify their ongoing detention'.[13] The federal government has restricted access to information regarding asylum-seekers and waged a concerted campaign to prevent them being personalised in any way. As Marr has noted, during late August and early September 2001 Peter Reith's press secretary, Ross Hampton, 'issued the famous direction to PACC [Public Affairs and Corporate Communication] not to take "any personalising or humanising images" of asylum seekers'.[14] It is this campaign to prevent the Australian people's appreciation of the humanity of asylum-seekers and their plight that Law's film is railing against.

As viewers we are brought to the point where we are anxious to meet Ali. The map tells us we have finally arrived in Port Hedland. The children wash off the slogans of freedom they have written on the car. We see the majestic mine of Port Hedland (reminiscent of Sue Brooks' *Japanese Story* – another film in which the foreigner is not allowed to remain in the Australian landscape). A sinister tension is introduced by the sudden appearance of police cars and vans. We are told of the pungent smell, the heat and the coating of red dust but we cannot appreciate such smell, such texture. Indeed Port Hedland and its brightly lit mine appear strangely beautiful, especially at night. Despite the earlier warning that no cameras or recording equipment are allowed inside detention centres, there is a somewhat unreal expectation that after all this time we will finally meet Ali. Our expectation is, of course, thwarted. We are offered a long camera shot across the centre's carpark of the family members walking along the perimeter fence and disappearing inside the gates. We have been jolted and shaken by the noise, dust and corrugation of the 'unsealed world', the 1000 kilometres of Tanami road, but at this moment we are more violently shaken by the closed nature of the sealed world, the world of detention in which Ali is imprisoned.

All we know about Ali at this stage, when we expected to know so much, is that he is not allowed out on day leave and the Kerbi family is forbidden to bring him pizza. But Law refuses to accept this sealing off. As she and Fong head back to Melbourne, we are offered 'more stories about Ali' – stories of abuse in detention, stories that demonstrate how truly removed from protection and basic human rights he is. Law sets Trish and Ali some 'homework', the term reinforcing the idea that this narrative is concerned with education. Trish and Ali are asked to speak about ancestors, the sea, suffering, death, anger, tears, dreams and home. In their responses we hear Trish's deeply resonant voice, in disturbingly stark contrast to Ali's silence, recounting her family connections, her teenage years, her sense of security and peace derived from her home. She says nothing on the subjects of suffering, death and anger. Ali has much to offer on these subjects and Law achieves something extremely important here: she communicates much of Ali's experience and feelings to us, yet she does not appropriate his story or attempt to speak *for* him. While we hear nothing directly from 'Ali', he is not, by this stage of the film, unknown to us. Law's filmic strategies have, in a sense, used the government's policy of censorship to achieve the opposite effect. Ali's absence and silence make us want to meet him more.

It is a wonderful moment, therefore, when we discover that Ali has been released from the centre and sent to community detention (though not to his family). The dramatic tension mounts as the Kerbis arrive in suburban Adelaide to meet Ali in freedom for the first time. The camera follows the family alighting from the car to greet him. Here Law's skill as a filmmaker is demonstrated most powerfully. Finally we are to see and hear Ali, but in place of a clearly focused shot of a teenage boy we have a heavily pixelated image. Such measures are legally necessary to protect the boy from identification and the threat of persecution if he were ever to return to Afghanistan, but while Law may be seen to be respecting this rationale, her strategy has a number of other effects. First, it frustrates the viewer and thus emphasises how the Australian government and, to a large extent, the media have sought to ensure that asylum-seekers remain faceless, nameless, voiceless. Second, it casts Ali as a ghostly spectre. As he wanders the Adelaide streets, plays on the beach, rides his bike, he is a shadowy presence who has the capacity to haunt the 'relaxed and comfortable' Australians he moves among. Third, Ali is a teenager, unrecognisable because he has been written over by the rhetoric of terror and fear.

In the closing stages of *Letters to Ali* Rob Silberstein's voice-over narrates the lifelong trauma suffered by his father, a man whose youth was taken because he was incarcerated by the Nazis. As we hear Rob's tale of his father's ritual cleansing in the waters off Adelaide, we observe the beauty and tranquility of an Adelaide beach being watched over by the haunted and haunting Ali. We do not know what the future holds for him. We know only that 'his freedom could end at any time'. In silence we read that if he loses his appeal to the High Court he could be locked up indefinitely or sent back to war-torn Afghanistan. Again Law destabilises us by presenting a glaring truth. We have been taken on this journey and have learnt to care about this particular boy, but she reminds us that his is 'just one of many stories' and that there are 'more stories waiting to be told'.

Law then plays her trump card. The caption tells us 'we are all waiting for a miracle', but there seems to be no hope in sight. It is then she remembers an epiphany she had on the first night of their journey out of Melbourne: a cloud-image of a mother dragon bringing her child home. We are shown this image and now we are equipped to understand it. Interestingly, it is on one level a Chinese image that we Australians, historically terrified of the invading 'Yellow Peril', are now comfortable and familiar with. This image, however, transcends all boundaries of race or ethnicity: it is an image of a mother and child. Law has been preparing us for this image from the outset. We remember at this moment how the newborn birds at the beginning of the film had their defenceless beaks raised in anticipation and trust towards their mother, and she fed them. We remember the many other images of motherhood in the film: Trish brushing Erin's hair, teaching Emma to knit, correcting Rian's homework, becoming Ali's Australian 'mum'. Trish's explanation of the miscarriage that prompted her need to become involved in writing to Ali takes on an added dimension. This film has been about educating its audience to see the fundamental issue at stake: children should be raised in a loving, safe environment, not in detention. One of the central journeys enacted in *Letters to Ali* is a journey towards ourselves; a journey through which we come to recognise a common humanity. We had been offered the beginnings of the mother/child dragon image twenty-five minutes into the film. The fully-formed image, however, was withheld until we had journeyed through the physical and moral terrain of post 9/11 Australia, until we had recognised the humanity of 'Ali' and understood our responsibilities to all those who flee trauma to seek shelter within our borders.

There was a time in this country when the White Australia Policy enjoyed almost universal support. It is difficult today for many young Australians to comprehend how a policy, now seen to be so offensive, flourished for so long. Perhaps there will come a time when the policy of indefinite mandatory detention also becomes incomprehensible to Australians. Perhaps *Letters to Ali* will become an historical text used to educate people about how different things were back then. For now, though, the film has a clear social purpose: to show Australia and its inhumane immigration policies to us and to move us to action. Law's style draws us into the film so that we become part of the process of discovery and we learn to recognise what is happening in our own country to people who come seeking asylum from terror. She opens up the lines of communication for us so that, if we choose to, we can ensure that those faceless, nameless people behind the barbed wire become so much more than 'a bunch of endearing letters and a voice at the end of the phone'.

An island home

Kim Scott

Last weekend a friend cooked me some abalone we'd plucked from the waters of one of the many bays along the south coast of Western Australia; one of those bays where you see the sun as it rises over the sea, or sometimes – depending on the time of year and where you sit – it rises over a strip of land beside that sea. It's the sort of place migrating whales sometimes strand themselves in, and in that way at least it's similar to the home of my indigenous ancestors a little further around the coast. So you'd think I'd know everything about its natural foods – its bush tucker. I don't. I was a bit embarrassed being shown how to prepare and cook that abalone.

You slash the strong, fleshy foot from the shell with a knife; next, scrub the sand and grit away, wrap a piece of cloth around the disc of sea-meat and bash it once or thrice with a hammer.

I'd stepped from the stale air of my motor car clutching eggs, a loaf of bread and some wine. I was looking forward to opening one of those bottles, but my friend insisted on me shivering in cold saltwater, bumping against slippery rocks, breathing through a gurgling pipe. I felt a bit like one of those stranded whales.

It seemed a very long time before we got to the wine.

I sipped further comfort from some research I'd been doing: indigenous people – that means Noongars here – never ate oysters, despite their abundance in many sheltered coves. Ships' crews pausing to resupply couldn't believe their good fortune and, writing about it in their logbooks, created such imaginative placenames as . . . Oyster Harbour.

They taste very different to abalone, oysters. I don't rate either of them, really. Edible enough, and certainly healthy: but so is all bush tucker.

We were camping on my friend's bush block. It's sea-change and tree-change country all at once: a granite headland, freshwater springs and clumps of trees towering in the granite's shelter from the prevailing cold, southerly winds. Dense bush spills down the steep slope to a crescent of sand. A couple of small islands sit a short swim from shore, and there's deep water between.

It's a refuge folded into granite rock not far from where the southernmost part of mainland Western Australia dives into the sea. A boat was built here in the early days of colonial Western Australia, and one time it was a shore-based whalers' camp. Cosy Corner, they call it, this grove of peppermints beside the Southern Ocean.

To most readers, it must seem a very long way from anywhere; we'd driven several hours from Perth, a city regularly joined to the phrase 'the most isolated in the world'. The bland placenames might even sound familiar: Perth, Cosy Corner . . . then there's Torbay Hill, Port Harding, Perkins Beach . . . You could be almost anywhere in the English-speaking world, surely. And those two islands so close to shore? Richards Island and Migo Island.

I recognised the name of the second island, or something very like it. In the nineteenth century Sir George Grey mentioned Miago, a Noongar man who had sailed with Sir Charles Darwin:

> The officers of the *Beagle* took away with them a native of the name of Miago, who remained absent with them for several months. I saw him on the North-west coast, on board the *Beagle*, apparently perfectly civilized; he waited at the gun-room mess, was temperate (never

> tasting spirits), attentive, cheerful and remarkably clean in his person. The next time I saw him was at Swan River, where he had been left on the return of the *Beagle*. He was then again a savage, almost naked, painted all over . . . Several persons here told me, – 'you see the taste for a savage life was strong in him, and he took to the bush again directly'. Let us pause for a moment to consider.
>
> Miago, when he was landed, had amongst the white people none who would be truly friends of his, – they would give him scraps from their table, but the very outcasts of the whites would not have treated him as an equal, – they had no sympathy with him, – he could not have married a white woman, – he had no certain means of subsistence open to him, – he could never have been either a husband or a father, if he had lived apart from his own people; – where, amongst the whites, was he to find one who would have filled for him the place of his black mother, whom he is much attached to? – what white man would have been his brother? – what white woman his sister? He had two courses left open to him, – he could either have renounced all natural ties, and have led a hopeless, joyless life among the whites, – ever a servant, – ever an inferior being; – or he could renounce civilization, and return to the friends of his childhood, and to the habits of his youth. He chose the latter course, and I think that I should have done the same.

Our retrospective view makes Grey's limitations obvious, but his honesty and high opinion of the Noongar man, Miago, is also obvious.

Miago would've been out of his territory this far south, but so often a 'guide', a 'native constable', or even an 'Assistant to the Government's Interpreter', he was accustomed to transgressing boundaries. Even so, I don't think he would've named an island after himself. That island may have been named in memory of him, but he didn't name it. The place-names he knew came from the language and stories of the first people to, in Jared Diamond's phrase, 'create a society in Australia'. Well, this part of it, anyway.

In Noongar – Cosy Corner's first language – the word for 'island' often translates as 'heart' or even, sometimes, 'knee'. Similarly, a hill is 'head'. This suggests that potential in this instance, expressed in roughly human form, is implicit in the landscape. It's a potentiality, awaiting a catalyst. And I reckon the catalyst is language.

What better way to appreciate the deeply human heritage of a place than by the language indigenous to it, the words and stories of its first society? Such words might even help a young, immigrant nation graft itself to the many older nations and older histories above which it shimmers.

Can that be done with justice?

We know that considerable damage has been done to our natural environment, and to indigenous languages. The map of 'Cosy Corner' shows very few placenames in Noongar language, other than an island that carries what may be the name of a Noongar man. The language is itself endangered; it has few fluent speakers, although at least there are more language teachers now than a few years ago.

Our shared history could be interpreted as designed to ensure that descendants of first societies don't know their ancestral languages, and don't know the placenames or stories they offer. In recent years I've tried to play a small part in reversing this. I like to call it 'language regeneration', but some prefer terms like 'resuscitation', 'reclamation', 'revitalisation' . . .

For me it means working with Elders to record and transcribe their language, and to identify its connection to the natural environment. It means going through archival language material with people who carry Noongar language. This is never an easy process: there are wildly variant spellings, there have been scribes with tin ears, there are words that contemporary Elders don't recognise. All of which can make the process unsettling, and even threatening. But it's also a joy to retrieve the voices of family you never heard speak, and to contemplate what they thought and felt and knew; to contemplate their world with them.

I'd like to say a little about a particular example of this. First, some background: eighty years ago an American linguist – Gerhardt Laves – visited one of the towns along our south coast and transcribed the stories of a number of Noongar men. When he went home, he took his paperwork – their stories – and began a completely different career path. After his death some notes were discovered in his attic and sent back to Australia sometime in the late twentieth century. A local university made his handwriting computer-friendly, and organised a community meeting to appoint a couple of representatives to help work out a 'protocol' for how to return the material to its community.

This was not as simple as it might appear. We tracked down descendants of the 'informants'. Sometimes this was very successful: we found a son and a daughter. They'd never really known their father; he'd died when they were very young and they were brought up in missions. One of them was an Elder in another part of the country. The surviving son of another informant, now in his eighties, was a well-respected Elder in our own region.

If there were no direct descendants, we found nephews and nieces. In some instances we could only locate grandchildren.

Eventually, we had a group of people who were descendants of Lave's informants, and also respected and well-grounded members of the Noongar community. We named them 'senior contact people' and they comprised a 'reference group' of about eighteen people, including a language teacher nominated by the majority of the group because of her skills and family connections. I use the phrase 'the majority of the group' because there were disagreements among us, particularly whenever we broached questions like:

- Who do the language and stories belong to?
- With whom should they be shared?
- What is the best way to do that?

The original 'informants' may well have been a single community, but there were jealousies and rivalries within our reference group, some with a long history, and we couldn't agree on every 'senior contact person'. Sometimes this was because, even if there was a genealogical connection, and even if an individual was recognised and accepted by the wider Noongar community and even perceived by many as an Elder, it did not follow that they were regarded that way by our small community of descendants, the reference group. Sometimes they, or an earlier generation of their family, may have been isolated from Noongar community in their youth, or even (allegedly) denied their Aboriginality and thus perceived to have not yet adequately restored their connection to community. In another instance, a person initially nominated as a 'senior contact person' and thought to be a direct descendant of one of the informants was challenged by others in the group who cited welfare files showing that her mother had been fathered by a non-indigenous man, not the man who had claimed her as his child and was directly descended from one of the linguist's informants. It was an argument, in many ways, about paper genealogies versus community acceptance and cultural knowledge.

Ironic: our arguments were conducted in English; and were a painful reminder of how oppressed communities turn on themselves.

Some of us in that group call ourselves 'social activists', and rally around slogans of social justice and the rights of indigenous peoples. In some ways our disagreements were more difficult to resolve than disagreements with the non-indigenous community, and at times I wondered if we'd become so accustomed to polemic struggle and conflict that we knew no other way of interacting with others.

Frankly, it's tiresome to recall our disagreements and their blustering intensity. Quite rightly, people wanted to know the stories and more of the language. Understandably, people saw status in being the gatekeeper of such material.

In the end, inevitably, the written protocol was a compromise agreed upon by a community of descendants. Upon its completion, a few people broke away, along with the documents they'd claimed, and those who remained were probably a stronger community because of it.

I make it sound very political; in truth, I hope such disagreements prove to be part of a longer process of community healing. Yes, there were raised voices and argument, and yes, there were tears. However, it wasn't only anger that caused those tears. Receiving the stories of your father, uncles, ancestors – even in a form you can't yet understand – can make you cry. Just holding a bunch of papers and plastic can strengthen your sense of who you are, and of continuity.

But is clutching them enough? Questions remain: Who owns the words and stories? Aren't language and stories communal? How, with justice, can these words be shared?

To a writer, publication seems the obvious answer. However, that would make the stories accessible to everyone, especially wealthy book-buyers with good literacy skills, two categories which feature, largely for historical reasons, few Noongar people. Therefore, publication might mean that those old-times storytellers speak to their own descendants only after everyone else has heard their stories of the place in which they live. Consider the historical context: indigenous people being displaced from land, dispossessed and disempowered. You wouldn't want publication repeating anything like that.

Surely, justice requires words and stories be returned to, and consolidated in, a community of descendants, and shared from there.

Nevertheless, our group remained interested in publication because it would provoke interest – both within and outside our community – in our heritage and language, and give an opportunity to initiate further projects.

We planned to publish only a very few stories, inspired by archival stories. This would involve three workshops.

The first was intended to give 'senior contact people' and their invitees an overview of the material and to make them more familiar with at least some of it. Hopefully, their enthusiasm and support would create enough momentum for us to succeed.

The second workshop was designed to give individuals an understanding of the principles of story illustration, and a further opportunity to become familiar with the selected stories.

The third workshop was intended to celebrate the return and consolidation of language and stories. We'd inform people associated with our 'community of descendants' of the process we'd followed, exhibit the art created by the illustration workshop, read the stories aloud, and give selected individuals – particularly those involved in formal or community-based education – photocopies of the texts and CDs of them being read. We hope this contributes to the 'return and consolidation' of the stories, encourages language regeneration, and improves career and/or employment prospects for at least some of our people by making them 'experts' on the stories before they're published.

The workshops would be part of the process of publication. Participants would gain a sense of 'ownership' of the stories, and we would gain some experience on how to conduct the similar future projects.

The first workshop began with 'senior contact people' being presented with 'their' stories in booklet and computer-disk form. It was very emotional; recipients and many in the audience cried because of this tangible return of stories and language. It occurred to some people there that it was unusual for so many of us to come together, other than for the too-frequent funerals.

We'd gathered at a camp in the bush beside a river not far from the town where the linguist had collected the stories. At most there would have been about fifty people present at any one time over the course of the weekend. People came and went; cars left and returned with a different set of passengers.

Across the floor we'd spread large sheets of paper on which, using the linguist's alphabet, I had written some of the stories chosen by the relevant 'senior contact person' and myself. Beneath each word I had also written its approximation in contemporary Noongar orthography and an approximate English translation. One page at a time, I attempted to read them aloud to a small circle of Elders on chairs around me as others beyond that circle observed, wandered away, moved in closer. People gathered in small groups outside the room, talking about what was happening, speaking Noongar language where they could. Then they'd come back inside to observe a little more.

It was intense in that circle, working out those stories. We recorded the Elders correcting my mispronunciations, and also their elaborations and digressions. Sometimes there were words or instances of language with which the Elders were not familiar. Not that they always agreed among themselves. Some of my generation, moving outside the circle of Elders and into my vision, signalled a break using the basketball 'time-out' signal.

In 'time-out' they emphasised what I was only half-aware of: the circle of elderly people was being dominated by those few with good hearing and able to read the strange alphabet; some were competitive enough to confront their peers (let alone the deceased linguist and upstart workshop facilitator); others of a more gentle temperament looked like they were getting ready to slip away.

We started again a little later, and over the weekend the membership of the groups changed slightly from one session to the next.

And so the weekend proceeded: elaborating from scrappy documents, recovering the sounds of an ailing language, imagining and realising the stories. Lines on paper faded; stories grew. We felt encouraged to continue with our plan, although one 'senior contact person' became upset going through her father's story, and so we withdrew it from the workshop process. It was just too much for her, she said, to be hearing her father's words.

For the second workshop we employed an established book-illustrator, Frane Lessac. We wanted another story-sharing opportunity, and a chance for people to get involved and try their hand at illustration. With luck we could identify illustrators for publication from among our own community.

At the third workshop . . . Well, as I write, the third workshop hasn't happened yet. Are we running out of energy? True, one of our core people is recovering from a kidney transplant, and others have taken on the care of even more family members. It's also true that we're doing this independent of institutional support and with limited funding.

We intend the third workshop to be a celebration of the stories and our process. We'll exhibit the artwork and read the stories aloud. We'll hand out paper copies and audio-recordings of the stories, and reiterate our process. We want our people to know the stories before they're ever published, to feel involved and complicit, and interested in participating in any similar, future process that leads to genuinely sharing our heritage with an increasingly wider audience.

A very significant part of that heritage, Noongar language offers a profound relationship with our natural environment and human history, and insights into another way of being. There's justice in hearing it from the descendants of the people who first created human society here, and in helping those voices be heard. Language must be shared to be alive, and speaking-and-listening is no crude giving-and-taking. It's more mutual: an investment in ourselves.

Writing: Seeking justice and truth amidst the imperfect good and the necessary

Frank Brennan

I received a phone call from Yusef Hussein. We had never met. He was a 36-year-old Palestinian born in Lebanon. After some years in Papua New Guinea, he was apprehended in a small boat in the Torres Strait. Australian immigration officials then flew him to the Christmas Island Detention Centre. Obviously well-educated despite his disrupted, peripatetic life, he told me that there was a small library in the Christmas Island facility. The staff were friendly, but there were very few inmates at the time and the isolation was killing him. In the library he discovered a copy of my book *Tampering with Asylum*.[1] He read it and thought I might be able to help him with his case. The immigration officials not only gave him permission to phone me but they facilitated the call and the transmission of key documents. Ultimately I met with his case officer and received the usual sequence of bureaucratic letters in response to my representations to the Minister. Yusef now has a visa and is settled in suburban Australia.

As an author, I have always been delighted when an audience member at one of my talks in a community hall thanks me for writing because the books and articles have helped her to inform herself and to be impassioned to act for justice. But I have rarely experienced the unexpected jubilation that welled up in me when Yusef told me that he had read my book. The book was about people like him, but it was not intended for them as readers. I had hoped that others reading the book might be more persuaded of the need to respond favourably to people like Yusef. Although I had delivered copies to the staff and inmates of the Baxter facility because I had often visited there and some of the stories related to that place, I had no idea that such a book would be permitted at or would find its way to the Christmas Island facility. Someone had gone to the trouble of placing the book in the Christmas Island library. Other government officials and contract staff had decided to leave the book available. And Yusef had decided to read it. The written word had provided hope and perhaps one step on the road to justice, out of the labyrinth of offshore immigration detention.

As an advocate for justice, I am asked why I write. The answer is because I never know who will ultimately read my written words nor how they will be assisted by them in their search for justice. Now I am confronted with another question: why would I write about why I write? I want to go deeper in giving an account of myself, hoping that the community of writer and readers might be enlivened and might move closer to justice and truth. To one's critics, giving an account of oneself can be a pointless exercise in self-justification. To those readers who find the writing helpful, the account can give further focus to the work for justice.

In 1995 I attended the international human rights course at Georgetown University in Washington DC. The professor, Robert Drinan, was a Jesuit priest and lawyer – as am I. After treating any topic, he would turn to me in a half mocking tone and ask, 'And how do you deal with this down under, in Australia?' Initially, I thought he was an American imperialist convinced that the United States always found the best way of addressing any human rights question; and while the United States had the answers, the rest of us were playing catch-up. But over the course of the semester, I realised that Drinan, who had travelled the globe extensively, had no preconceived notion about the best way of achieving justice. It all depended on the local circumstances. There were principles to espouse and to act upon in the search for any solution. We became friends. He died in January 2007. At his funeral, the preacher made this observation:

> Any society built on the practice of rights is not so sweetly transcendent as the holy mountain of feasting and joy which Isaiah summons up for us; it is not so intimately and delicately responsive as the virtue of charity or agape which St Paul commends to us. But it is essential to the realisation of the common good in a world which is marked by enormous human diversity and intermittently intense social conflict. It is a reality which protects those of us who are neither beasts nor angels from our own worst impulses and from the harms which others would do to us. It is not the realm of the best but of the imperfect good and the necessary.[2]

As a public advocate for social justice, I am convinced that writing is an indispensable way of seeking justice and hoping for truth in the realm of the 'imperfect good and the necessary'. While all participants in the political process have their 'take' on truth in the process and justice in the outcome, we never quite reach them, though they are our destination. Mathematicians use the concept 'asymptote' – the straight-line axis on a graph with curved lines on either side verging without touching the axis, even if the curved lines stretch along the axis to infinity. Justice and truth are asymptotic in those instances deserving political debate. We never quite reach the perfect articulation of them. Of course, there are many instances where truth is articulated and justice achieved and thus there is no need for political deliberation, but heightened political controversy occurs precisely because there is no consensus about justice or truth. In searching for a political solution, the public needs to be educated; politicians need to be accountable; and the voiceless need to find a voice, preferably their own.

An advocate has his place, but his writing stands on its own, taking on a life of its own – text waiting to be appropriated or rejected by other political actors seeking the lines of those asymptotes. My passion for writing is in helping readers move towards those asymptotes. I do not write about situations in which I think there is no prospect of my moving conflicting parties or the general public any closer to the asymptotes of justice and truth or where there is a risk that such writing will cause harm without any corresponding benefit to those who have been wronged. Situations like Papua and Timor come to mind.

The first seeds of my political consciousness sprouted precisely at 8 am on 3 February 1967. I was twelve years old and had just been promoted to the large dining room at my country boarding school. Breakfast started at 7.45 am. The din of 300 boys at table was always deafening. For the first and only time in my five years at the school, a handful of senior boys called for a minute's silence; this minute's silence at 8 am was to mark the hanging of Ronald Ryan in Melbourne Jail. As Ryan dropped, you could hear a pin drop in faraway Toowoomba, Queensland. The recollection still brings goose bumps. This hanging was wrong. It should never happen again. How could a nation do this? All Australian jurisdictions then abolished the death penalty. My adolescent moral sensibilities found resonance in public debate, law reform and policy change. Values and principles mattered.

The second significant political event in 1967 was the constitutional referendum of 27 May when Australians voted overwhelmingly to amend our Constitution so that the Commonwealth Parliament could make laws for the benefit of Aborigines and Torres Strait Islanders. There was a strong expectation that the discrimination and exclusion of the past would be put behind us and that Indigenous Australians would see themselves as having an assured place at the political table, especially when their own interests were at stake. Given my later involvement in Aboriginal affairs, I would love to have a recollection to share of that event. But I have none. As far as I know, I had never met an Aborigine. Breakfast and every other meal that day proceeded without silence or variation at my boarding school in Toowoomba. On some issues, we were ignorant.

Ten years later, I had studied law and politics in Brisbane. The Queensland premier, Joh Bjelke-Petersen, announced: 'The day of the political street march is over.' He told student activists not to bother applying to the police for a permit, as they would not get one. For two years police then exercised their discretion wrongly, in accordance with the premier's wishes. Two thousand people who went to the barricades were arrested. Ultimately there was a change of government and the law was amended, guaranteeing the right of public assembly. Public political protest bore results. Arguments about civil liberties affected the policies of at least one of the major political parties. Moral wrongs could be put right. The actions and opinions of young people mattered. Even in the wake of Sir Joh's populist politics, values and principles mattered. It was time to write.

I published my first book, *Too Much Order with Too Little Law*, in 1983.[3] During the late 1970s, I had been engaged as a barrister to appear for demonstrators who had been arrested. Often the demonstrators were convinced that their right of public assembly should be unqualified and that it was improper for police to regulate political protest even if it interfered with the regular traffic flow. The politicians and the media were adamant that there was no right of public protest and that ordinary Queenslanders should be allowed to go about their lawful daily business in the centre of the city without disruption from people whose only purpose was to draw attention to themselves. I did not find either side of the argument completely compelling. Each had a point. There was a need for a law and a policy which struck a more appropriate balance, and they were not going to eventuate from protests alone. Bjelke-Petersen's political strength was his consistency. He never backed down. He had a finely tuned sense of what the ordinary voters thought about university students who had nothing better to do than to protest. The protesters invoked lofty philosophical arguments in support of their right to protest at will, quoting international human rights charters. Seeking a middle course, I argued the case for judicially reviewable discretion of the police officers charged with the task of granting permits for protest marches. I made an historical study of the Queensland law and policy and did a comparative analysis of other jurisdictions, thereby making the case that at other times and in other places in Australia it was possible to recognise a right of public protest, regulated so as to have due regard for the legitimate expectation of protesters and of other citizens who might be disrupted by such protest.

Once conflict on the streets had died down, there was a need for coherent public argument for the right of public protest. Law reform would not come quickly without a development of community understanding, because the Labor Party in Opposition knew that the premier's populist appeal would increase were they to advocate law reform or a stricter review of police discretion. When the Goss Labor government was elected, the Electoral and Administrative Review Commission appointed me its adviser on public assembly laws. The Commission's report was adopted by government and the Queensland Parliament passed the *Public Assembly Act*. All this took some years, but it was heartening to have one's first book bear fruit in providing public education, policy change by a major political party and ultimate law reform. There was a point to writing about legal issues primarily for a non-legal audience, and there was a point to writing about policy questions without taking a party political stance. Change on the back of rational discourse was possible even in populist Queensland. I was not so foolish as to think my book was determinative in the change, but it was a contribution and my authorship provided the entrée to the political process of reform.

I then spent sixteen years agitating for Aboriginal rights in Australia, publishing numerous articles and four books on the topic: *Land Rights Queensland Style*,[4] *Sharing the Country*,[5] *One Land, One Nation*[6] and *The Wik Debate*.[7] When writing on Aboriginal issues, because I am not Aboriginal, I have first and foremost wanted to give an account of myself, in light of my participation in the political processes, seeking legal and policy change. It has been important for me to eyeball the decision-makers and those most adversely affected by their decisions. It has also been important to educate the public while giving a public account of myself. Prior to *Mabo*, there were very few resources available for lawyers to visit remote Aboriginal communities in states like Queensland and to hear first-hand the concerns of Aboriginal occupants on remote reserves. I was generously invited to learn from and speak with Aboriginal communities across the country.

My introduction to the legal and political issues of Aboriginal rights came in 1981 when I was junior counsel in the Alwyn Peter case in Queensland.

Alwyn was the fifteenth Aboriginal male in three years to have killed another Aboriginal person on an Aboriginal reserve. In these cases, the victim was usually the accused's partner, and so it was in this case, Deidre Gilbert being the victim. Senior Counsel, Des Sturgess, thought this could be the ideal test case on diminished responsibility for Aborigines living on Queensland reserves who had been charged with the murder of their companions. We called leading experts in anthropology, psychology, psychiatry and sociology. Just prior to trial, the Crown indicated its willingness to accept a plea of guilty to manslaughter rather than murder. Our expert testimony could then be more quickly provided to the court by way of mitigation on the question of punishment.

Sturgess told the court:

> In Queensland there have been created communities in which the incidence of homicide and very serious assaults is among the highest recorded and published in the world. To be a member of such a community one does not have to be bad or mad. One only has to be Aboriginal.

In each case, the accused and the victim were shaped by life on a reserve, and each in their own way was destroyed by it. We defence lawyers had a good win in the Peter case. Alwyn walked free within weeks of the completion of the court proceedings. A woman anthropologist left me with the chilling observation that our forensic win had removed the one inadequate protection for defenceless women in remote Aboriginal communities – the minimal deterrence of the whitefella legal system. After the case, I received the last letter that the anthropologist W. E. H. Stanner ever wrote:

> I am fascinated by the question: how do general ideas about human conduct change so quickly? I can recall about fifty years ago appearing as a witness for the defence in an Aboriginal murder case in Darwin before Justice Wells. He was notably unimpressed by my arguments but nevertheless reluctantly took them into account in mitigation,

while looking round the court as if expecting trouble. Or do I mean 'remarkably quickly'?[8]

After Alwyn walked free, Paul Wilson published *Black Death, White Hands*. David Bradbury and Tony Strachan then got to work. I had spoken to David Bradbury who was shooting a documentary entitled *State of Shock*, but I did not have any detailed discussion with Tony Strachan who wrote the play of the same name. I attended a performance of *State of Shock* at the Belvoir Theatre in 1986. The program carried some of the transcript of the Alwyn Peter court proceedings, including my examination of one of the witnesses. It was a surprise to read my name oft-repeated in the transcript. It was a shock then to see the onstage presentation of the lawyer, who in Act Two, Scene 1, gruffly visited the prisoner named Eddie Thomas in his cell at the Townsville Jail, dropping oranges on the floor and then telling him, 'You've had your thinking time, Eddie. Now it's time to talk. Talk, Eddie. [*Pause*] Fuck, eh? [*Pause*]. You're up on first degree, mate. They're out to get you, to put you in a box like this for life. Understand?'[9]

This gruff style was not mine. I thought that I and my instructing solicitor, Peter Clapin, had proceeded very respectfully and tentatively in all our dealings with Alwyn. But how violent and incomprehensible was the legal process despite our best efforts to explain it? How inconceivable and irrelevant were many of the questions we were asking of Alwyn? Just as I was stereotyped in the play, so too was Alwyn. A play reduced to two actors taking on various personae demands such starkness. The message of justice could be communicated only by overlooking the complexity of the truth. Morality, law and politics were conflated in one discourse. Dichotomies, contrasts and gaps between the lawyer and the prisoner in the cell were needed in the play, though my purpose in being in that cell in life was to bridge gaps and understand Alwyn's perspective.

In the bicentenary year, 1988, David Bradbury launched his documentary in Sydney. Alwyn and his mother, Rachel, featured in the documentary and travelled to Sydney for the gala event, together with Jean Jimmy who also featured in the documentary, having been the key local witness in the court proceedings, explaining the living conditions of Alwyn's family and community. During their time away from the Mapoon reserve, Alwyn's brother Sidney was charged with committing a very serious assault on a woman. This was not Sidney's first encounter with the law for such activity. Even prior to Alwyn's case, Sidney had stood trial for causing grievous bodily harm to his girlfriend Geraldine, who later took up with another man who killed her, having previously killed his wife. Geraldine's father had also been murdered. While Alwyn was making the national headlines, his brother was back home being taken into custody for the same sort of violence we had sought to explain in the case. Explanation did not necessarily entail justification or excuse; understanding the explanation did not necessarily result in community acceptance or forgiveness. Through the law, society expressed a more ready understanding of why people like Alwyn and Sidney assaulted their women. In part, the state was responsible for the policies that resulted in such community living conditions. Our advocacy and the artistic expression of Strachan and Bradbury highlighted the institutional wrongdoing by the state; in the shadows the moral guilt of Sidney and Alwyn played out.

I was committed to land rights and local self-determination for Aboriginal communities. Unlike the perspective in Strachan's play, I never saw land rights and self-determination as the panacea for a utopian Aboriginal future on remote communities. However, I thought (and still do) that land rights and local self-determination were essential preconditions for Aboriginal communities starting to put their lives together with some dignity in a post-colonial situation. Through my writing, I saw myself as having a role in helping to lift the yoke of past (and continuing) oppression. I had no illusions that the mere recognition of land title or the granting of local self-government would transform the lives of people like Alwyn, Sidney, Deidre and Geraldine. Not being Aboriginal and not working constantly in one Aboriginal community, I had no expectation that I could do anything further, other than fostering a spirit of reconciliation between Aborigines and other Australians, once that yoke was lifted.

The two major national debates on land rights in which Aborigines have had a place at the table of negotiation have been the native title debates of 1993 and 1998. At a critical time in each debate, the key Aboriginal protagonists fell out with the chief non-Aboriginal politician with whom they were negotiating. In 1993 that politician was Paul Keating, and in 1998, in view of Prime Minister Howard's intransigence and the state of the parties in the Senate, it was Brian Harradine. In neither 1993 nor 1998 was there a perfect answer to what should be the content of native title legislation. Justice was asymptotic. Neither was there any agreement about the outcomes at various stages of the legislative negotiation process. Truth was also asymptotic. Keating's frustration with the Aboriginal negotiators boiled over in 1993 when he declared, 'I am not sure whether Indigenous leaders can ever psychologically make a change to decide to come into a process, be part of it, and take the burdens of responsibility which go with it.'[10] The Aboriginal negotiators' frustration with Harradine boiled over once Noel Pearson retracted, without coherent reasons, his public endorsement of Harradine's negotiated compromise with John Howard.

There is always a need to distinguish what law is desirable from what law is achievable. Thus the mix of principle and pragmatism. The pursuit of justice requires moral, political and legal discourse. Detailed legal precision may help the public discourse, but it is just as likely to cloud the moral assessment and distract from political strategy. Given that I have often enjoyed access to decision-makers (and that access might not have been so readily available to those most affected by a law or policy), I have always seen a need, in justice, to give a transparent account of myself in so far as this can be done without violating confidences. During the 1998 *Wik* debate, a considerable amount of my correspondence with politicians and key stakeholders was leaked on two occasions to Alan Ramsay at the *Sydney Morning Herald*, highlighting that some of my direct representations to decision-makers would not usually be intended for publication at the time of negotiations. I have often seen publication *post facto* a useful tool of public accountability.

My political opponents sometimes regard my writing as insufficiently academic or legal. In a public debate about law and policy, there is a need for acute legal analysis, but that is usually confined to the legal fraternity. The Howard government would never be convinced to extend Aboriginal land rights in response to a learned legal article. I have always insisted in my public justice writings that you take seriously the government of the day and its policy agenda, and you take seriously the views of the majority who are likely to be cowered by fear, suspicion and ignorance about minority rights and claims. I have always been committed to writing books, articles and opinion pieces for the general public, in the confident hope that unless the case can be made comprehensible to the ordinary punter there is little prospect of elected governments legislating benignly for unpopular minorities like Aborigines and refugees. Public fear is a political bonus for some governments. That fear can be driven out only with accurate information and non-partisan empathy. During the 1998 *Wik* debate, I visited many pastoral properties in western New South Wales and Queensland. I was especially grateful to the angry pastoralist who told me that I should go back to my Sydney church and say my prayers. He clarified my thinking.

An issue as complex as *Wik* could not be resolved by prayer alone; it could not be resolved by calling only stakeholders to the table; and it could not be resolved just in the big cities. There was a need for some citizens who were not Aborigines, miners or pastoralists to participate in the public conversation in country towns and on pastoral properties, assisting with the resolution of conflicting claims. When addressing a diversity of audiences who are the protagonists in a national dispute, it is essential that one's key proposals are put in writing so that all parties have access to the same perspective.

I have been able to go in hard on occasion because I do not represent a particular constituency. In negotiations, government will often leave the door open on a proposal, with the result that parties can be misled into thinking that the proposal is still on the table. I count my writing most helpful in those situations when it causes government to come clean. Even if government made no response to such publication, I would be well placed to restate my interpretation, with the observation that without a constituency I could be contradicted readily by government without causing offence to others.

In both *One Land, One Nation* and *The Wik Debate*, I thought it important that I give a *post facto* account of the negotiations and the outcomes consistent with the discussions to which I had been party, not because mine was the only perspective but because mine was not a self-interested perspective, in the sense that I was not representing Aborigines, mining companies or pastoralists but was seeking an optimal compromised outcome that honoured principles set down by the key political actors. This has always been a vulnerable position, with my writings being subject to three significant criticisms: (1) He appears to speak for Aborigines and sells them short; (2) He advocates only a soft left, symptom theory; and (3) His writing does not pass muster in the legal academy. One benefit of now writing about why I write is that it provides a public opportunity to respond to such criticisms.

Sometimes there has been a perception that I speak for Aboriginal people. During the 1993 native title exercise, Noel Pearson offered a very enlightening public critique of my public *modus operandi*:

> I always have a go at Frank for being too cynical about politicians. Sadly, white politicians seem to find it easier to talk about Aboriginal issues with someone like them. It's more comfortable for them to talk to someone like Frank than to come and talk to us. He's a very influential player, and if he suggests the middle ground as the position for politicians to take, then what actually happens is less than that. I think he doesn't realise how much weight white politicians put on his imprimatur. He tells them what they can get away with. It's important that he doesn't aim too low, because inevitably he will get less than he asks for, and it can drag the aspirations of the Aboriginal people down. Still, I am always saying that if black people think Brennan is striking an unacceptably conservative position, then it's up to them to articulate how a less conservative position might work.[11]

As a writer, I can agitate only for what I regard as the just outcome. On the Pearson view, I should agitate for more than that, so that a just outcome might result from the ensuing political compromise. From Pearson's perspective, my approach could yield only an outcome less than justice. If I were to take the Pearson approach, over time my readers (including politicians) would surely discount my writing to offset the inflated demands for the less advantaged group in a political dispute. During the 1998 *Wik* debate, Aden Ridgeway, on behalf of the National Indigenous Working Group, wrote to the *Sydney Morning Herald*:

> There is no doubt that Fr Brennan has immense respect and affection amongst Aboriginal people throughout the country. More significantly, he is widely listened to by Australians generally because he is believed to speak for Aboriginal people. This has created a desperately difficult dilemma for Indigenous leaders. Fr Brennan's support and advocacy are much needed; but where he takes a stand which differs from that of Aboriginal people themselves, especially over difficult issues of political judgment, the very fact that he is believed by the general community to speak for Aborigines suggests that he should be silent on such topics.[12]

The second criticism has been Noel Pearson's concern that I write as an apologist for the symptom theory in Aboriginal affairs with a soft-left-liberal approach:

> The Alwyn Peter case became a cause celebre, and Brennan made his mark with it. The whole approach was to paint Alwyn Peter (who had murdered his girlfriend whilst drunk) as a victim of history, trauma, Mapoon removal etc. etc. The symptom theory underpinned the whole view – and has underpinned the whole 'social justice' approach to Indigenous problems with the criminal justice system from the Peter Case to the Royal Commission into Aboriginal Deaths in Custody and to this day. Where has this whole approach taken us in the last 25 years in terms of the breakdown of social order and the spiralling problems?[13]

More the issue is that there are many topics in Aboriginal affairs that I have not written about and will not. It is not my place and I profess no expertise about how Aboriginal leaders and Aboriginal communities should conduct themselves once the historic injustices of dispossession and colonial subjugation have been corrected in law and government policy. I do not involve myself in internal Aboriginal disputes and neither do I write about them. I write only at the interface between Aborigines, the law and government policy.

Alwyn Peter deserved a lesser penalty for a dreadful crime because he lived in an adverse social situation that impacted on his behaviour, and that social situation was in part caused by racially discriminatory laws and the policies of the state. He still deserved some punishment for the killing of Deidre Gilbert. There is a need on those Aboriginal communities for policies and programs that are able to deliver better social outcomes, especially in the face of chronic substance abuse, child abuse and long-term unemployment. I applaud advocates like Noel Pearson who dedicate their efforts to suggesting and experimenting with such programs. The fact that I do not write publicly about such programs or agitate for them (other than to urge government to be attentive to the local voice of Aboriginal communities and their leaders) should not be taken as subscription to a symptom theory about Aboriginal community life. There were (and still are) symptoms of Aboriginal life caused by past unjust laws and policies which have needed to be put right. But the relief of those symptoms is only the beginning of building cohesive Aboriginal communities, a task that is primarily the responsibility of Aboriginal leaders and those whose professional assistance they seek.

The third criticism was best articulated by Nick Bolkus for the Labor Party during the *Wik* debate. He told the Senate:

> [Brennan's] statements and writings of fifteen or so years ago provided a benchmark for social and legal comment in the debate. The impact of his work was positive and quite often courageous. But much has changed over recent years, and the roots that we are talking

> about – over some fifteen or so years – have been developed. The breadth and quality of academic debate, and academic lawyers writing in this field, have grown exponentially.
>
> The particular problem that we now have with the good father stems from the confusion as to what particular hat he may be assuming to be wearing. Is he an academic lawyer? Is he a theologian and a moral guide? Or is he, as is often the case, a political commentator and lobbyist? If you were to look at his recent writings in not just the public press but also in learned journals, you can identify a certain range of characteristics. Unfortunately, I think one of those characteristics is that he has become increasingly dismissive of contrary opinions, heavily reliant on citing his own statements and his own previous writings to justify his conclusions.
>
> The fact is that his work has tended to be critically viewed more in the way that one would approach Father O'Malley's Sunday sermon sometimes than as a serious work of contemporary and legal relevance.
>
> I think Frank has played a valuable role, and he has a valuable role to continue to play. As a priest, I think he has a right and a duty to comment on moral issues. As a political commentator, he can line up with the army of other hopefuls in that growing band of commentators. But let us recognise when he does give legal advice, that, as a lawyer, he is one among many . . . I think, for the sake of Father Brennan's flagging reputation, he should also tune in to some of the writings of eminent counsel and maybe move on as well.[14]

A writer like me is stung at the time by such criticism. But the writing stands. Justice demands moral, political and legal discourse. The learned Silk's opinion stands for little when elected legislators are contemplating how to strike the balance between conflicting rights. Well-informed political analysis is not enough to convince government of the need to protect minority rights when such rights collide with economic development as well as the rights of others close to government (like miners and pastoralists). Father O'Malley's Sunday sermon is never enough to swing the balance, but it may provide the foundation for a political analysis and legal opinion that can work some slight rectification in the name of justice. Evoking such criticism may be a sign that one is close to the mark in political and social commentary. At least, the criticism makes it more difficult for the government to discount Fr O'Malley's remarks as the thinly disguised opinion of the Opposition parties.

There is a whole legal discipline that has evolved around native title. It does not much interest me, because I am not a lawyer employed by newly resourced Aboriginal groups staking their native title claims under the legislation first passed in 1993 and amended in 1998. Senior Counsels providing learned legal opinions to politicians during the legislative process is about as useful as politicians providing party manifestos to the High Court. My primary target audience has not been lawyers and native title aficionados. My audience has been the general public and the politicians effecting the compromises at the time. In 1998 when the criticism was made, there was a bevy of lawyers retained by the Aboriginal groups and the Labor Party crafting detailed amendments to John Howard's proposed amendments. In the political process, the fate of those amendments rested with Brian Harradine in his face-to-face negotiations with the prime minister. The bevy of lawyers had not only provided Harradine with the amendments but had also provided him with a hierarchy of issues that needed to be brought to the table. The prime minister then named a handful of key sticking points during the second Senate debate. Harradine in turn then negotiated with some of the Aboriginal leaders and with the prime minister over those sticking points. In July 1998 Harradine delivered what the National Indigenous Working Group (NIWG) unofficially supported back in April 1998. I wrote congratulating him and agreed to his publishing the letter. It was necessary that the public understand that Harradine had delivered and that the prime minister had backed down considerably between the second and third Senate debates. My subsequent writing on the issue was consistent with Noel Pearson's accurate assessment that Harradine had won the penalty shoot-out four–nil on the four key sticking points.[15]

It took some years for Harradine's critics to concede that he had improved Howard's land rights package more than was originally hoped for. Seven years later, when Harradine was retiring from the Senate, Andrew Bartlett, deputy leader of the Democrats, made this acknowledgment of Harradine's acumen on *Wik*:

> The agreement he reached on the *Wik* legislation was one of the few cases I would point to where John Howard was bested in negotiations. Whilst the legislative merits of the *Wik* agreement were less than ideal, the sort of race election, focused on Indigenous people, that our country would have faced in 1998 if that agreement had not been reached would have been far worse even than the one we endured in 2001.[16]

These were complex political issues and I still have a strong self-interest in agitating a particular view of it all. But without resolving all the outstanding questions, one needs to ask: Would it have been good enough in 1998 for one in my position simply to critique the Howard legislation without working to create the space for Harradine to effect a compromised outcome which was more beneficial to Aborigines, and at the same time avoiding the prospect of a race-based election? Having critiqued the Howard legislation, I could have withdrawn from the political fray, arguing that the world of political controversy is no place for a writer and commentator (who is not a stakeholder or politician), especially when the controversy is marked by a sharp contest between political parties, after all stakeholders have put their case to the public.

Whatever the internal contradictions of the High Court's *Wik* decision, I believed that the decision delivered to Aborigines a right to negotiate with mining companies wanting access to traditional lands that were also subject to pastoral leases. The government was wrongly claiming that equal treatment of Aboriginal native title holders and pastoralists required that native title holders had no right to put their case about the effects of mining on their sacred sites and other areas of land used for residence or traditional activities. The Aborigines' own lawyers had crafted a compromise on the right to negotiate. Rather than withdrawing completely from the political process, I thought it right to create the space and pressure for government to accept that compromise, thereby avoiding the need for the legislation to be held over until a subsequent election, when a returned Howard government would have been more emboldened to legislate without the compromise crafted by lawyers for the NIWG.

Often the decision requiring greatest discernment is *whether* to write rather than *what* to write. I first visited East Timor in November 1992, a year after the Santa Cruz massacre. I went with the firm intention of returning to Australia and saying nothing publicly. But on my last night in Dili, Bishop Belo took me to a party where I met Mario Carrascalao who had been governor of East Timor. The two of them urged me to return to Australia and speak and write publicly, but under no circumstances was I to speak or write about the need for independence. They did not think it achievable and they thought that such talk simply made the situation more difficult for the young people who were unwilling to accept the inevitability of their situation. They urged that I confine my public utterances to three issues: the need to reduce the Indonesian military presence; the need for greater respect for human rights in East Timor and greater supervision of human rights violations by the Indonesian authorities; and the need for greater cultural autonomy in the province.

I returned to Australia and kept faithfully to the text. There were many church and NGO people in Australia who thought I was guilty of appeasement. I had been to East Timor. I had seen the situation. Surely I was obliged to speak strongly about the Timorese right of self-determination. Such a morally pure stance by me might have resulted simply in greater suffering and bloodshed for people in East Timor, threatening the people I had spoken to. It was not my life at risk. It was not my blood that would be spilt.

Now I fast-forward from Dili in 1992 to Jayapura or Manokwari in Papua in 2007. What do I do? What can any of us say or write? No doubt the so-called act of self-determination supervised by the UN in 1969 was a sham. But applying the same principles as I applied in East Timor, I will keep silent unless and until I hear from those whose lives are on the line, those whose blood will be spilt in any fight for self-determination. If anything, I will be even more cautious, hopefully not because I am growing more conservative but because the parallels with East Timor highlight greater problems. East Timor was costing Mr Habibe US$100 million per annum from the Jakarta coffers. The Freeport mine in the Papua province is Jakarta's largest single taxpayer. Of the two million people in the two Papua provinces, there are 800 000 transmigrants from other parts of Indonesia, and they are the majority of the business class. East Timor was always left on the unresolved list of the UN General Assembly. The UN signed off on the integration of West Papua as part of Indonesia more than thirty years ago. The UN is not in the habit of reopening questions about the territorial boundaries of member states. Papuan independence groups do not have an international network of their own people advocating independence at the highest levels on the diplomatic cocktail circuit. Inching towards the asymptotes of justice and truth, the most I can do for Papua at this time is to write why I do not write. All I can responsibly do at this time is to visit Papua and listen to the voices, faithfully publishing only what they ask of me, as their words may well be written in their blood.

I spent fifteen months working in East Timor after independence. But I saw no case for my publicly critiquing the fledgling Timorese government or the misconceived UN gestures at reconciliation in substitution for the establishment of a functioning judiciary, police force and serious crimes unit. Rather I confined myself to writing about the injustice of Australia's proposed oil and gas deal in the Timor Sea, welcoming a more just outcome when Foreign Minister Downer reopened the negotiations offering a revenue split of 50–50 rather than 82–18 in favour of Australia. Being an Australian, not a Timorese, it was important for me as a writer not to cause offence or to add difficulty to the task of government by indigenous leaders seeking to establish a new nation from the ashes of the 1999 conflagration.

It may be because I write cautiously, attempting to respect diverse viewpoints, that I am asked to publish my thoughts on issues in which I profess no particular expertise. This can be problematic. I accepted the invitation from the Council for Christians and Jews (NSW) to address the Kristallnacht Commemoration in Martin Place on 10 November 2006. Alas, my text was not written and it caused great hurt to some of the Jewish audience. Here is the unchallenged recollection of the part of my text that caused offence:

> Imagine hearing the sound of that broken glass in the street that night and knowing that they were coming for you. Imagine smelling the smoke of destruction that night and knowing they had marked out your family – not because they knew you personally, not because they had anything against you individually, but because of your race, because of your religion. Thus began the horror of the Holocaust. Once they knew, everyone pledged, 'Never again. Never again.' That pledge seems to have gone up in smoke, drowned out by the smashing of the glass whether it be in Rwanda or Darfur, in Iraq with Kurds, Sunnis and Shias hating and killing each other just because of race or religion.
>
> Wanting to honour the memory of this dreadful event, I asked Jewish colleagues committed to universal human rights what an Australian Christian should say all these years later. They urged me to reflect on the universality of the problem and the signal lesson for all humanity that any repetition of discrimination and persecution on the basis of race or religion should shock us all. We should not caricature groups or people different from us. We should be careful about name-calling.
>
> Just last year I made my first visit to Jerusalem, the holiest of cities. One afternoon an Australian rabbinic scholar who is an old friend showed me over the Old City. That evening I travelled with a Palestinian Christian through the newly constructed wall, through the checkpoints to the ghetto-like conditions of Bethlehem. It pains us all that there is division on the basis of race and religion even in the holiest of cities. In our present situation here in Australia, we are painfully aware that the other great Abrahamic religion is not with us at such a commemoration. With fears of terrorism, it is those different

> from us in race or religion most likely to be suspected of terrorist activity. But we are people of hope.
>
> As we contemplate the horror of the broken glass and the stench of the smoke, we remember those whose homes, businesses and places of worship were destroyed that fateful night. Sixty-eight years on, we pledge ourselves with hope to be people committed to universal human rights for all, regardless of race or religion. No matter how dark and difficult it be, let's recall the simple words of hope of Ann Frank, 'How wonderful it is that nobody need wait a single moment before starting to improve the world.'

Rabbi Jeremy Lawrence thought that in a 'grotesquely offensive' way I was wanting my listeners clearly to infer 'an analogy with the concentration camps or of a parallel between Hitler's persecution of the Jews and Israeli policy to Palestinians'.[17] I did not draw any such analogy and neither did I want my listeners clearly to infer any such analogy. I too would find such an analogy grotesquely offensive. I promptly published an apology and wrote to Rabbi Lawrence, noting:

> Given the high risk of hurtful misunderstanding by Jewish participants, it was unwise to make reference to the contemporary situation in the State of Israel. Be assured my concern is for all innocent peace loving persons living in the State of Israel, regardless of their race or religion.[18]

Rabbi Lawrence published this response:

> I had a very positive meeting with Fr Brennan on Friday morning in which he presented a very sincere and unreserved apology for the hurt occasioned by his remarks at the CCJ Kristallnacht Commemoration. I believe that Fr Brennan understands why his remarks were taken to be inappropriate. Fr Brennan reconfirmed that he had not set out to draw any analogy with the Holocaust and that he finds any such comparison

> repugnant. I greatly appreciate the honourable way that Fr Brennan addressed the situation and his constructive contribution to interfaith dialogue.[19]

Rabbi Raymond Apple wrote from Jerusalem, unconvinced:

> I would not let Father Brennan off the hook so soon or so easily. A speaker has to know what to say and where, when and how to say it. To be blunt, Father Brennan had no idea what to say and was amazingly ill-advised to come to a solemn commemoration of the Holocaust without first informing himself of the nature of the occasion and the sensibilities involved. His attempt at apologising is inadequate. He needs to give an undertaking to speak out of knowledge, not ignorance, on every future occasion that he has to give an address on any platform at all.
>
> Further, I strongly advise him to think, say and do nothing in relation to Jews, Judaism, the Holocaust and Israel until he has read the books of Professor Abraham Joshua Heschel, Rabbi Joseph Ber Soloveitchik and Rav Avraham Yitzhak Kook.[20]

There are some issues in which justice and truth are not only asymptotic but are beyond the shared horizon of speaker and listener, writer and reader. One cannot abandon hope but one must speak and write only out of the shared pain of the differing perspectives. I was devastated to learn that my well-intended words had caused offence at this solemn occasion. If I could unwittingly cause such harm, there is every prospect that many other Australian Christians could cause similar offence without malice or any intention to abuse or to be distasteful. It was unwise for me to give the address without first insisting on a meeting with members of the Council of Christians and Jews. It was also unwise of me not to have an address in writing. I wonder whether the knowledge base demanded by Rabbi Apple is one directed towards the asymptotes of justice and truth, or only one drawn from the Jewish perspective. Even at a contemporary Kristallnacht commemoration there should be a place for the respectful word embracing the universal cry 'Never again, Never again'. Any discrimination and persecution on the basis of race or religion should shock us all.

In a democracy, the citizen is entitled to engage freely in public disputation about the contested manifestations of justice and truth. The writer who becomes a player in the political process has no privileged access to justice or truth. Controversies marked by religious sensibility, cultural sensitivity, racial discord and fundamentally divergent views on the good can move more readily towards resolution when the writer is able to articulate the penumbra between the contested views about values, self-interest and ideology, and the asymptotes of justice and truth. After thirty years in the public forum, I do not find writing in and about this space any easier. That may be because we are now facing some of the more intractable questions about justice and truth, and because we do not share a common perspective even on the position of the asymptotes. The reader who is assisted in more boldly staking a claim for the place of justice and truth in the clouded political contest of the day is the one who provides ultimate inspiration for this scribe to keep writing of the imperfect good and the necessary.

Acknowledgments

I wish to thank the contributors to this collection, all of whom made time in their busy schedules to write these essays for what they deemed a worthwhile cause. My appreciation also goes to UQP, particularly Madonna Duffy for her immediate and unfailing enthusiasm for the project, to Wendy Sanderson for her diligence and professionalism and Felicity McKenzie for her insight, precision and friendship.

Notes on contributors

Frank Brennan

Frank Brennan is a Jesuit priest and law professor. His books on Aboriginal issues include *The Wik Debate*, *One Land One Nation*, *Sharing the Country* and *Land Rights Queensland Style*. His books on civil liberties are *Too Much Order with Too Little Law* and *Legislating Liberty*. His book *Tampering with Asylum* compares Australia's asylum policies with those of other developed countries. His latest book, *Acting on Conscience* (2006), explores how law, religion and politics can be responsibly mixed. Frank is an Officer of the Order of Australia (AO), which recognises his services to Aboriginal Australians, particularly as an advocate in the areas of law, social justice and reconciliation. He and Patrick Dodson shared the inaugural Human Rights Award presented by the Australian Council for Overseas Aid (ACFOA). He was awarded the Humanitarian Overseas Service Medal for his work in East Timor and the Australian Centenary Medal for his service with refugees and human rights work in the Asia–Pacific Region.

Jane Harrison

Jane Harrison, a Muruwari descendant, is a researcher and writer. Her play *Stolen* premiered at Playbox Theatre in 1998, followed by seven annual seasons in Melbourne, with tours to Sydney, Adelaide, regional Victoria, Tasmania, the United Kingdom (twice), Hong Kong and Tokyo, plus readings in Canada and New York. *Stolen* has been on the VCE English and New South Wales HSC syllabi and was a co-winner of the 2002 Kate Challis RAKA Award. Jane's play *On a Park Bench* was a finalist in the Lake Macquarie Drama Prize. She contributed a chapter to *Many Voices: Reflections on Experiences of Indigenous Child Separation* (NLA). Her play *Rainbow's End* premiered in 2005 in Melbourne, had a production in Tokyo in March 2007, and was published in *Contemporary Indigenous Plays* (2007). Jane was the 2006 Theatrelab Indigenous Award Winner for *Blakvelvet*, and in 2007 she won the Peter Holmes a Court Indigenous Award for her latest play, *Can White Girls Dreamtime?*, now titled *Custody*.

Anita Heiss

Anita Heiss is from the Wiradjuri nation of central New South Wales. Her published works include an historical novel, *Who Am I? The Diary of Mary Talence, Sydney 1937*, a chicklit novel, *Not Meeting Mr Right*, a poetry collection, *I'm Not Racist, but . . .*, a children's novel, *Yirra and Her Deadly Dog Demon*, a satirical social commentary, *Sacred Cows*, a non-fiction text, *Dhuuluu-Yala (To Talk Straight): Publishing Aboriginal Literature*, and a literacy reader entitled *Me and My Mum*. In 2003 Anita was awarded the Australian Society of Authors Medal (Under 35s), and she won the Deadly Award for Outstanding Achievement in Literature in 2007. Anita is currently Deputy Chair of the Australian Society of Authors, Chair of Gadigal Information Services and National Coordinator of the AustLit – Black Words subset.

Gail Jones

Gail Jones is both a writer and an academic. She currently holds a Chair of Writing at the University of Western Sydney and is the author of two books of short stories, *The House of Breathing* and *Fetish Lives*, and four novels, *Black Mirror*, *Sixty Lights*, *Dreams of Speaking* and the most recent, *Sorry*. Gail is also the author of a short monograph on the film *The Piano*, and writes academic articles on various subjects. Her fiction works have won numerous literary awards and have been widely translated overseas. She travels often and has been awarded writers' residencies in India, Ireland, the United States and France.

Peter Manning

Peter Manning began his career at the *Bulletin* under Donald Horne and then at the *Sydney Morning Herald* and the *Sun-Herald*, before becoming a television reporter of news and current affairs at the ABC on *This Day Tonight*. In the 1980s Peter produced programs such as 'The Big League' for *Four Corners*. After a period as executive producer of *Four Corners*, Peter became head of ABC News and Current Affairs and introduced programs such as *Lateline*, *Foreign Correspondent* and *Landline*. In the 1990s he took over as general manager of ABC Radio National and later joined the Seven Network as an editorial executive. In 2000 Peter became Adjunct Professor of Journalism at the University of Technology Sydney. He has lectured in investigative journalism, television and specialist reporting. He undertook a PhD and has published part of his research in *Dog Whistle Politics and Journalism: Reporting Arabic and Muslim People in Sydney Newspapers*. In September 2007 Random House published his latest book, *Us and Them: A Journalist's Investigation of Media, Muslims and the Middle East*.

Adrian Martin

Adrian Martin is a Senior Research Fellow in Film and Television Studies, Monash University, Melbourne. He is the author of *The Mad Max Movies* (Currency/Screensound 2003), *Raúl Ruiz: Sublimes Obsesiones* (Altamira 2004), *Once Upon a Time in America* (British Film Institute 1998) and *Phantasms* (Penguin 1994), as well as forthcoming books on Brian De Palma (Illinois University Press) and Terrence Malick (BFI). He is the editor of *Movie Mutations: The Changing Face of World Cinephilia* (BFI 2003) and *Film – Matters of Style* (Continuum 1992) and the co-editor of the Internet film magazine *Rouge* (www.rouge.com.au). He has regular columns in *Cahiers du cinéma: España* (Spain), *De Filmkrant* (Holland)

and *Film Quarterly* (USA), and his essays appear in publications including *Trafic* (France), *Sight and Sound* (UK), *Undercurrent* (magazine of the International Federation of Film Critics) and *Tren de sombras* (Spain). He has won the Pascall Prize for Critical Writing and the Australian Film Institute's Byron Kennedy Award.

Noel Rowe

Noel Rowe was a poet, critic and Senior Lecturer in Australian Literature at the University of Sydney. He has published three collections of poetry, *Perhaps After All* (Vagabond 2000), *Next to Nothing* (Vagabond 2004) and *Touching the Hem* (Vagabond 2006). Noel died on 11 July 2007. His *Collected Poems* and critical essays will be published by Vagabond Press in 2008.

Eva Sallis

Eva Sallis is fiction and non-fiction writer. Her award-winning novels include *Hiam* (Vogel and the Dobbie Literary Awards), *Mahjar* (Steele Rudd Literary Award 2004) and most recently *The Marsh Birds* (Asher Literary Award 2005). Eva has co-edited several anthologies, most recently *Dark Dreams: Australian Refugee Stories* and *No Place Like Home: Australian Stories*. She has a PhD in comparative literature. She studied Arabic for many years and travels regularly to the Middle East. She has published translations from Arabic, including *Two Banks with No Bridge*, a chapbook of Yahia' al-Samawy's poems. Eva is co-founder and current president of Australians Against Racism Inc. (AAR), a group made up of volunteers and skilled professionals who donate their time to projects in arts, education and the media that counter prejudice. As part of AAR's current projects Eva coordinates Ozarabic, an Arabic language and culture course for children, and, with Gillian Bovoro, coordinates Adnyamathanha Ngawarla Yarramalka, an Aboriginal language and culture course for children and adults.

Kim Scott

Kim Scott is a Noongar man. His first novel, *True Country*, was published in 1993. His second novel, *Benang*, won the Western Australia Premiers' Literary Prize 1999, the Miles Franklin Award 2000 and the RAKA Kate Challis Award 2001. Kim's most recent book, *Kayang and Me* (2005), was written with Noongar Elder Hazel Brown, and is based on her oral history of their community.

Rosie Scott

Rosie Scott is an internationally published, award-winning novelist, essayist and short story writer. She was appointed a permanent member of the Council of the Australian Society of Authors and received the Sydney PEN award and a Human Rights nomination for her work with refugee writers. She is co-founder of Women for Wik. Her latest novel, *Faith Singer*, was included in an international survey of '50 Essential Reads by Living Writers' conducted by the *Guardian* Orange Prize Committee and the Hay Writers Festival.

Katherine Thomson

Katherine Thomson began her career in the theatre as an actor. Her plays have been performed by Australia's leading theatre companies and include *King Tide, Harbour, Mavis Goes to Timor, Wonderlands, Navigating, Diving for Pearls, Barmaids, A Sporting Chance, Darlinghurst Nights, Kayak* and *This Hospital Is My Country*. Her television writing credits include *Satisfaction, Answered by Fire, Blackjack, Grass Roots, Wildside, Fallen Angels, Halifax fp, GP* and *Something in the Air*. She was awarded the 2005 New South Wales Premier's Literary Award for *Harbour* and has won seven AWGIEs and the Louis Esson Prize for Drama in the Victorian Premier's Literary Awards. Katherine is a past president of Sydney PEN and has been active in the Australian Writers' Guild for many years. She was the recipient of the 2003 Rodney Seaborn Playwright's Award, and in 2005 received the Australian National Playwrights Centre award for her substantial contribution to the Australian theatre industry.

Endnotes

Introduction

1 'Literature, transformation and unease', *Australian School Library Association Journal*, vol. 18, Issue 1, 2004. http://www.asla.org.qu/pubs/access/a_commentary-180104.htm

2 Henry Porter, *Observer*, Sunday, 18 March 2007.

3 *At The Same Time: Essays & Speeches*, Paolo Dilonardo and Anne Jump (eds), Farrar Straus Giroux, New York, 2007, p. 115.

4 Dorothy Green, *The Music of Love: Critical Essays on Literature and Life*, Penguin, Ringwood, 1984.

Art in a time of crisis

1 In *Griffith Review*, Summer 2006–2007, pp. 13–60.

In praise of political fiction

1 *Sydney Morning Herald*, 21 October 2006.

2 Kurt Vonnegut, *Wampeters, Foma and Granfalloons: Opinions of Kurt Vonnegut*, Delacorte Press/Seymour Lawrence, New York, 1974.

3 *New Zealand Listener*, 5 March 1990.

4 Alejandro Murguia (ed.), *Volcan: Poems from Central America: A Bilingual Anthology*, City Lights Books, San Francisco, 1984.
5 Rebecca Solnit, *Hope in the Dark: The Untold History of People Power*, Text, Melbourne, 2005.
6 Frantz Fanon, *The Wretched of the Earth*, MacGibbon and Kee, UK, 1965.

Just poetry

1 Martin Buber, *I and Thou*, trans. Ronald Gregor Smith, Charles Scribner's Sons, New York, 1958 (second revised edition, with a postscript by the author), p. 63.
2 Eva Johnson, 'A Letter to My Mother', in Kevin Gilbert (ed.), *Inside Black Australia*, Penguin, Ringwood, 1988, p. 24.
3 The poems are taken from Judith Wright, *Collected Poems 1942–1985*, Angus & Robertson/HarperCollins, Sydney, 1994, abbreviated as CP with page references supplied in the essay.
4 Kath Walker was the first Indigenous writer to break into mainstream publication. Her *We Are Going* (Jacaranda Press, 1964) is one of the most significant moments in Australian literature. In 1988 she changed her name to Oodgeroo.
5 Rosemary Dobson, *Collected Poems*, Collins/Angus & Robertson, Sydney, 1991. References are to this edition, abbreviated as CP.
6 See Dobson's Preface to her 1973 *Selected Poems*, reprinted in *Selected Poems*, Angus & Robertson, Sydney, 1980.
7 D. McCooey, '"Looking into Landscape": The Elegiac Art of Rosemary Dobson', *Westerly*, 40, 1995, pp. 15–25; and D. McCooey, 'Rosemary Dobson: Vision and Light', *Rosemary Dobson: A Celebration*, National Library of Australia, Canberra, 2000, pp. 61–68.
8 John D. Caputo is a deconstructive theologian. He is the author of, among other works, *The Tears and Prayers of Jacques Derrida*.
9 John D. Caputo, *Against Ethics*, Indiana University Press, Bloomington and Indianapolis, 1993, pp. 72–73.
10 Thomas Aquinas, *Summa Theologiae*, 1a2ae.56, in *Selected Philosophical*

Writings, ed. and trans. Timothy McDermott, Oxford University Press, Oxford, 1993, Oxford's World Classics, pp. 398–409.

11 *The Merchant of Venice*, IV.i.191f, William Shakespeare, *The Complete Works*, ed. Peter Alexander, Collins, London and Glasgow, 1966 [1951 Tudor Edition]), p. 246.

12 Francis Webb, *Collected Poems*, Angus & Robertson, Sydney, 1977. References are to this edition, abbreviated as CP.

13 William Shakespeare, *The Complete Works*, ed. Peter Alexander, op. cit., p. 1004.

My journey through *Stolen*

1 R. Scobie, Aborigines Protection Board, NSW Parliamentary Debates, 27/1/1915.

2 Source unknown.

3 Letter from James Isdell, Travelling Protector, Kimberleys, to Charles F. Gale, Chief Protector of Aborigines, Western Australia, 1909.

Speaking shadows: Justice and the poetic

1 Quoted in Amy Colin, *Paul Celan: Holograms of Darkness*, Indiana University Press, Bloomington and Indianapolis, 1991, p. 49.

2 This is Pierre Joris's translation of Paul Celan's 'Speak, you too', in Pierre Joris (ed.), *Paul Celan: Selections*, University of California Press, Berkeley, 2005, pp. 54–55.

3 The phrase 'thinking with grief' is quoted by Geoffrey Hatmann in *Scars of the Spirit: The Struggle Against Inauthentification*, Palgrave, London and New York, 2002, p. 83.

4 Robert Manne, *In Denial: The Stolen Generations and the Right*, Shwartz Publishers, Melbourne, 2000, pp. 15–21.

5 Giorgio Agamben, *The Coming Community*, trans. Michael Hardt, University of Minnesota Press, Minneapolis, 1993.

6 This is Jacques Derrida's phrase, cited in Thomas Keenan's *Fables of Responsibility: Aberrations and Predicaments in Ethics and Politics*, Stanford University Press, Stanford, 1997, p. 37.

7 Joseph Brodsky, 'An Immodest Proposal', in *On Grief and Reason*, Farrar, Straus and Giroux, New York, 1995, p. 211.

8 This is a claim made for essays in the wonderful book *Loss: The Politics of Mourning*, David L. Eng and David Kazanjian (eds), University of California Press, Berkeley, 2003.

9 This is the persuasive view of Kathleen A. Gill in 'The Moral Functions of an Apology', in Rodney C. Roberts (ed.), *Injustice and Rectification*, Peter Lang, New York, 2002, pp. 111–23.

10 This is quoted in Jill Robbins' essay 'Visage, Figure: Speech and Murder in Levinas's *Totality and Infinity*', in Cathy Caruth and Deborah Esch (eds), *Critical Encounters: Reference and Responsibility in Deconstructive Writing*, Rutgers University Press, New Brunswick, 1995, pp. 275–98.

11 This is Jerome Rothenberg's translation in Pierre Joris's *Selection*, p. 46.

12 Celan, quoted in Paul Auster, 'The Poetry of Exile', in *Paul Auster: Collected Prose*, Faber and Faber, London, 2003, pp. 351–59, at p. 354.

Boring humanist bodies

1 Roland Barthes, 'Writers, Intellectuals, Teachers', in *Image-Music-Text*, Fontana, Glasgow, 1977, p. 199.

2 Bill Krohn, '*Les Cahiers du cinéma* 1968–1977: Interview with Serge Daney', *The Thousand Eyes*, no. 2, 1977, p. 20.

3 ibid., p. 22.

4 David Williamson, 'Culture Crusade a Sideshow', *Australian*, 9 October 2006, p. 14.

5 Mathias Lavin & Stéphane Delorme, 'Petit arrangements avec le jeune cinéma français', *Balthazar*, no. 3, Autumn 1998, p. 28 (my translation).

6 Bill Krohn, '*Les Cahiers du cinéma* 1968–1977, p. 23.

Aboriginal children's literature: More than just pretty pictures

1 Treat: Awards for Excellence in Educational Publishing, <http://alex.edfac.usyd.edu.au/TREAT/centre_awards_2002.html>.

2 NSW Ministry for the Arts, <http://www.arts.nsw.gov.au/awards/HistoryAwards/2002%20Hist/2002awards.htm>.

3 Susan Allen, 'Papunya Tula – The Birthplace of Contemporary Australian Aboriginal Art', <http://www.wsws.org/articles/2001/aug2001/tula-a24.shtml>.

4 ibid.

5 NSW Premier's History Awards: <http://www.arts.nsw.gov.au/awards/HistoryAwards/2003Hist/2003awards.htm>.

6 Jackie Huggins, inside cover endorsement, Mary Malbunka, *When I Was Little, Like You*, Allen & Unwin, Crows Nest, 2003.

7 Alice, 11 years old, Adelaide, <http://www.yara-online.org/reviews_04/when_little.htm>.

8 Edna Tantjingu Williams and Eileen Wani Wingfield, *Down the Hole – Up the Trees, across the Sandhills . . . Running from the State and Daisy Bates*, Jukurrpa Books, Alice Springs, 2000, p. 2.

9 ibid., pp. 12–14.

10 ibid., p. 48.

11 ibid., p. 42.

12 Doris Kartinyeri, illustrated by Kunyi June-Anne McInerney, *Bush Games and Knucklebones*, Magabala Books, Broome, 2003, p. 27.

13 Robyn Templeton and Sarah Jackson, illustrated by Robyn Templeton, *Tell Me Why*, Magabala Books, Broome, 2004, p. 12.

14 Rhonda Black, email to the author, 2 March 2007.

Writing for performance: Privilege, politics and goose bumps

1 Rachel Fensham and Denise Varney, *The Dolls' Revolution: Australian Theatre and Cultural Imagination*, Australian Scholarly Publishing, Melbourne, 2005. p. 159.

2 *Wonderlands*, Currency Press, Sydney, 2004.

3 A. M. Duncan-Kemp, *Our Channel Country*, Angus & Robertson, Sydney, 1962; *Where Strange Paths Go Down*, W. R. Smith and Paterson, Brisbane, 1952; *Where Strange Gods Call*, W. R. Smith and Paterson, Brisbane, 1968.

4 Henrietta Walmark, 'Pick of the Day', *Globe and Mail*, 10 September 2006.
5 *The Search for Signs of Intelligent Life in the Universe*, Harper & Row, New York, 1986.

Travelling towards ourselves: Rights and recognition in Clara Law's *Letters to Ali*

1 Clara Law, '*Letters to Ali*: Personal Journey, Political Cinema: a talking film seminar held as part of the Melbourne International Film Festival 2004', included as an extra on *Letters to Ali* DVD, distributed by the AV Channel Pty Ltd.
2 Trish called the boy 'Ali' to protect his identity.
3 John Grierson, *Grierson on Documentary*, Forsyth Hardy (ed.), Faber and Faber, London, 1966, p. 13.
4 David Marr, 'Is the Media Asleep?', in Robert Manne (ed.), *Do Not Disturb: Is the Media Failing Australia?*, Black Inc.Agenda, Melbourne, 2005, p. 221.
5 Roland Barthes, 'The Photographic Message', in Stephen Heath (ed. and trans.), *Image/Music/Text*, Hill and Wang, New York, 1977, p. 26. Also, we need only to remember the captions, such as that from Melbourne's *Herald Sun*, 'Overboard: boat people throw children into the ocean', which accompanied the photos of the rescue crew of the *Adelaide* saving 223 men, women and children from the sinking *Olong*. The photos had been sent out from the *Adelaide* with the captions 'Courage' and 'Courage and Determination' (David Marr and Marion Wilkinson, *Dark Victory*, Allen & Unwin, Crows Nest, 2003, p. 193).
6 This supposed division between 'us' and 'them' was powerfully shattered when news broke that Cornelia Rau, an Australian citizen suffering from schizophrenia, had been incarcerated mistakenly at Baxter detention centre. Shortly after, it was revealed that the government had deported Vivian Alvarez, another unwell Australian citizen, to the Philippines.
7 Michael Freeman (ed.), *Lloyd's Introduction to Jurisprudence*, 7th edn, Sweet & Maxwell, London, 2001, p. 50.

8 H.L.A. Hart, 'Positivism and the Separation of Laws and Morals (1958)', in *Lloyd's Introduction to Jurisprudence*, 7th edn, Sweet & Maxwell, London, 2001, p. 368.
9 David Marr, 'Is the Media Asleep?', p. 222.
10 ibid.
11 David Marr and Marion Wilkinson have remarked upon the 'exquisite irony' that Captain Banks, the commander of the *Adelaide*, was ordered to prepare to leave for the Middle East, but before he 'could join the operation against the Iraqi dictator he first needed to stop a boatload of Iraqis fleeing Saddam from setting foot on Australian soil' (*Dark Victory*, Allen & Unwin, Crows Nest, 2003, p. 190).
12 Natascha Klocker and Kevin M. Dunn, 'Who's Driving the Asylum Seeker Debate? Newspaper and Government Representations of Asylum Seekers', in Helen Wilson (ed.), *The New 'Others': Media and Society Post-September 11*, Media International Australia incorporating Culture and Policy No. 109, Griffith University, Nathan, Qld, 2003, p. 77.
13 ibid., p. 78.
14 David Marr, 'Is the Media Asleep?', p. 218.

Writing: Seeking justice and truth amidst the imperfect good and the necessary

1 Frank Brennan, *Tampering with Asylum*, University of Queensland Press, St Lucia, 2003 (2nd edition, 2007).
2 J. Langan, Homily, Gonzaga Church, Washington DC, 1 February 2007, available at <http://www.law.georgetown.edu/>.
3 Frank Brennan, *Too Much Order with Too Little Law*, University of Queensland Press, St Lucia, 1983.
4 Frank Brennan, *Land Rights Queensland Style*, University of Queensland Press, St Lucia, 1992.
5 Frank Brennan, *Sharing the Country*, Penguin, Melbourne, 1991 and 1994 editions.
6 Frank Brennan, *One Land, One Nation*, University of Queensland Press, St Lucia, 1995.

7 Frank Brennan, *The Wik Debate: Its Impact on Aborigines, Pastoralists and Miners*, University of New South Wales Press, Sydney, 1998.
8 Letter of Professor W. E. H. Stanner to author, 4 October 1981.
9 Tony Strachan, *State of Shock*, Currency Press, Sydney, 1986 (revised edition 2000), p. 35.
10 P. Keating, Press Conference, 8 October 1993, quoted in *One Land, One Nation*, p. 66.
11 Quoted in M. Simons, 'Father Figure', Good Weekend Magazine, *Weekend Australian*, 11–12 September 1993, pp. 38–39.
12 Letter to the Editor, *Sydney Morning Herald*, 6 March 1998.
13 N. Pearson, 'A Fair Place in Our Own Country: Indigenous Australians, Land Rights and the Australian Economy', Castan Public Lecture, Castan Centre for Human Rights Law, Monash University, June 2004.
14 (1998) CPD (HofR) 5122–3; 7 July 1998.
15 Noel Pearson told the ABC's *7.30 Report* on 1 July 1998: 'It looks on the face of it, in this penalty shoot-out situation, Brian Harradine's won four-nil. Full credit to Senator Harradine for having promised us that he was going to hold the line. He's surely held the line. He's held out on a stubborn position. It appears that Senator Harradine has substantially saved the position that will give Aboriginal people procedural rights on pastoral leases, which from one point of view at least looks like a right to negotiate under a different guise.'
16 (2005) CPD (S) 142; 21 June 2005.
17 Letter of Rabbi Jeremy Lawrence to the Council of Christians and Jews (NSW), 10 November 2006.
18 Letter of author to Rabbi Jeremy Lawrence, 12 November 2006; repeated in public apology to Rabbi Jeremy Lawrence and any other persons offended by my remarks at the Kristallnacht Commemoration, The Great Synagogue, Sydney, 17 November 2006.
19 Statement of Rabbi Jeremy Lawrence to the Council of Christians and Jews (NSW), 20 November 2006.
20 Letter of Rabbi Raymond Apple to *Australian Jewish News*, 24 November 2006.